Looking Beyond the Rearview Mirror

Looking Beyond the Rearview Mirror

Writings from the heart

E.T. BIDDIX

Copyright © 2020 E.T. Biddix

The right of E.T. Biddix to be identified as the author of this work has been asserted by them in accordance with the Copyright, Designs and Patents Act 1988.

All rights reserved. No part of this publication may be reproduced, transmitted, or stored in a retrieval system, in any form or by any means, without permission in writing from the publisher, nor be otherwise circulated in any form of binding or cover other than that in which it is published and without a similar condition being imposed on the subsequent purchaser.

Names: Biddix, E.T., author

Lowery, Rosalie, editor

Title: Looking Beyond the Rearview Mirror / E.T. Biddix

Identifiers: ISBN 9798680378458 (Paperback)

Cover design by Teressa J. Martin/TJM Cover Designs

Contents

Dedication	i
In Memory	iii
About the Author	v
A Note from the Author	viii
CHAPTER 1	**1**
Y'all Eat Yet, Come on In, Eat and Talk a Spell	2
Mountain Talk	3
Little Switzerland Store	4
How Do You Want Your Eggs??	6
Spit and Whittle Club	6
Coffee	7
Mountain Cookin'	8
The Country Store on Grassy Creek	9
Mom and Pop Stores	10
Birthdays at Our House	11
Walnut Cake	12
CHAPTER 2	**14**
Mountains and Relatives – Forever With Us	15
Family Tree	16
The Blue Ridge Mountains	16
Faye Lowery Biddix (My Mother)	17
Helen and Burl	19
Johnny Simmons	21
Pauline Susan Biddix (My Sister)	23
Aunt Nell	24
Esther, A True Lady	26
Aunt Duskey	28
Bobby and Ted	29

William Douglas Biddix (My Little Brother)	32
CHAPTER 3	**33**
My Dad, My Hero	34
Daddy, Grandpa, and Christmas	35
Belts	37
Dad and the War	37
Cutting Wood	39
Honest Work	40
Eyes in the Back of His Head	41
What Fair??	41
Dad and Football	42
Chain Reaction	44
Dad and My First Car	45
Medals in the Closet	46
My Dad, LAX, and Johnny Cash	47
CHAPTER 4	**50**
Grandpa John Lowery – A True Man of the Mountains	51
John Alexander Lowery	52
Grandpa and the Constitution	53
Grandpa on the Go	54
Grandpa the Weatherman	55
Grandpa vs. the Government	56
Grandpa, Tobacco, and Me	57
Grandpa, Watching Girls Go By	58
Ice Cream and Grandpa	59
Way Over in Madison	60
Grandpa's Birthday	61
Grandpa's Wooden Coffin	63
Goodbye Grandpa	64
CHAPTER 5	**66**

Faith is Fundamental	67
A Follower That Fails	68
A Conversation With God	68
Revival in the Mountains	69
Thank God for Unanswered Prayer	71
An Angel at Sam's Club	72
God's in the Skyscraper	73
I Haven't... However...	74
Prayer	75
A Sore Throat From Heaven	76
Hats in Church	77
The Inward Voice	78
The Face of God	79
The Least of These	80
Christians Without a Conscience??	81
CHAPTER 6	**84**
My Misspent (But Fun) Youth	85
An Encounter That Lasted a Lifetime	86
Game Day, October 1960	87
Coach John Norton	89
Pappy Broadway	91
Curfew	92
Guilty, Your Honor	93
Mistaken Identity	95
Stella	96
Shoot Again Sheriff	98
Blue Devils, Bulldogs, and the Sheriff	99
Friday Night Lights	101
The Play	102
The Smoking Corner	103

Petticoat Malfunction	104
The Girl on the Bus	105
Football and Life	107
One Little Mistake	108
The Center	109
The Pile	110
Ice Water Toting in Hell (Fall, 1960)	111
Finger Lickin' Good	112

CHAPTER 7 — 114

Life Just Became Complicated	115
Margaret Willis Biddix	116
Tommy Aaron Biddix	117
Bobby Travis Biddix	118
Aaron Morgan Biddix	119
FBI	121
1964 Chevelle	122
Aaron's Eyes	123
Double-A	124
Rocky	125
Coach Ed	126
My Son Can Pitch??	128

CHAPTER 8 — 130

Some Facts, Some Opinions	131
Opinions	132
Memorial Day	132
Majestic Oak	133
Worry	134
Children in Cages	135
Prejudice	136
Fading Away	136

I Cried Today	137
The Other Side of the Glass	139
War	140
Fall	141
Basketball and Golf	142
Sounds	143
One by One	144
The Least of These	145
CHAPTER 9	**147**
Work Stories, Intriguing People, and Events	148
Ali	149
George Adams Jefferson	150
Jamie—A Lesson in Courage	153
The Captain in Gucci Boots	155
Experiences	156
B-17	158
The Small Box	159
Marty Robbins	160
Nice Outfit Ma'am	161
Jet Fumes	162
The N-Word and the Country Music Star	163
Lake Greeson	164
Fall Fishing Finality	166
A TRUE Fish Story	167
They Come, They Go	168
Show Your Badge	169
Marty Stuart	171
CHAPTER 10	**173**
Friends and Friendships Matter	174
Old Friends	175

Real People	176
A True Friend	177
DP (Dave) Davis	178
WD Thomason	179
Larry Boyd	180
Mike Dennison	183
Bob Hyland	184
Dave Sneed	185
Norman (Mo) Holt	186
Horace Gaines	187
My Friend, Ed Hampton, Is Gone	189
Norman Ridenhour	191
The Three of Us, Joe, DP, and Me	192
Mrs. Tandy Cook	195
Don Ray Howell	196
Bob and Jewel Norris	198
My Friend, Bob Norris, Is Gone	199
The Queen	201
One Day	202
CHAPTER 11	**205**
A Little of This, A Bit of That	206
Age	207
Names	207
New and Improved!!??	208
The Forgotten	208
Real Men Cry	210
My Change, Please	212
Cross Out the Cat	213
Hoeing Corn	214
Junk, Memories, and Treasures	214

Crosscut Saw	216
Easy to Say, Hard to Do	217
Class Reunion of 1961	219
Battlefield	219
CHAPTER 12	**221**
The Circle of Life	222
A Legacy??	223
I Must Be Getting Old	224
Wayward Sons	225
The Operating Room	226
The Lady from Latvia	227
Fall Chills (and Hope)	228
The Elevator	230
Crutches, Walkers, and Handrails	231
Breakdown Blues	232
Diane and Teresa	233
Our Class	234
The Committee	235
What Do You Do??	236
Why Not Me?	237
See You Soon	239
What's the Purpose of It All?	240
The Wisdom of the Cherokee	241
Contemplation	242
No Tears	243
Acknowledgements	**245**
Author Bio	**246**

Dedication

Many people helped in the formation of this book. I appreciate every one of them, and their names appear on the front pages.

However, there is only one person on the planet I would ever dedicate my book, Margaret Willis Biddix. My wife, as of this writing, for fifty-seven years. Without her, I would never have taken pen to paper. Actually, without her, there would be no ET Biddix. She, in a sense, rescued me a long time ago, always believed in me, and because of her love and devotion to our family kept me away from the path I was on.

Margaret, the strongest person I know, is the epitome of a true Southern Lady. She loves God, family, and her fellow man. I have never seen hatred or prejudice from her in any form. A little bit of temper at times, though usually justified.

A few of the poems in this book will take you on a journey of how we met and about our life along the way. I dedicate this writing to my beautiful wife, lover, and friend, Margaret. She is also the mother to our children and a grandmother to our grandchild. She is the one that holds our family together.

I love you more than you could ever possibly know.

In Memory

Tommy and Faye Biddix
Burl and Helen Willis
William Douglas Biddix
DP (Dave) Davis

About the Author

Ed Biddix is a cherished friend of mine and has been for several years. We met years ago at Third Baptist Church in Murfreesboro, Tennessee, and I soon picked up on Ed's friendliness, his concern for others, and deep faith in God.

I found Ed to be a deep thinker, tolerant of my point of view, and over the years, we have had many conversations on a variety of subjects. Ed has what I would call a photographic memory, and I marvel at how he can tell a story in his poetry.

The reader of this book will find complete honesty in Ed's writings. He does not spare his embarrassing moments, and you will meet some interesting characters, enjoy some humorous stories, a bit of his philosophy and opinion. Other poems express Ed's faith, the ups, and downs of his life, but always mindful that there is redemption for those that believe and trust in God. I believe in the poetry of my friend, and you will find yourself saying yes, that reminds me of someone, been there, done that, I can't believe I did that, and so on.

And maybe this book will help you restore a lost friendship, be thankful for the past, live each day to the fullest, and face the future with renewed courage and faith. Enjoy!

Mike Dennison
Retired Professional Engineer

My friend Ed Biddix is from the mountains of North Carolina, where he encountered life with some of God's most interesting people. No matter their age, all of them enriched his life, and many challenged his mind toward a fuller life in Christ.

For the many years I have known Ed, he has served his Lord as a deacon minister, Bible teacher, and a faithful witness of God's Grace. The Holy Spirit, who indwells in him, has made him an excellent communicator of divine truth. You will discover special insights as you digest the joyful thoughts of his writings and poems of truth.

WD Thomason
Pastor and Friend

I first met Ed Biddix 40 years ago on his many trips to Washington when times seemed more civil, and life was simpler. Reading his book about people, places, and his faith was a pleasant journey back to that era.

Bart Gordon
Member of Congress (1985-2011)
Tennessee, 6th District

I have known Ed Biddix for the past 16 years. We attend church together, and

I have the privilege to work alongside him in ministry. He has always been faithful in his teaching and to minister to those in our congregation that are unable to attend and in need. Ed has gone on many trips to help in Disaster Relief with our biggest effort coming after Katrina in New Orleans. Ed headed up our Disaster Relief team for three years, making trips to New Orleans, New York, Oklahoma City, and numerous Tennessee locations. I am thankful to Ed for his friendship and encouragement to me. One of the truly good guys we have today.

Steve Hutson
Pastor, Third Baptist Church
Murfreesboro, TN

I have had the pleasure of working with Ed. as his Financial Advisor for more than 17 years. Over the years, that relationship has become one of true friendship. Ed has shared some of his work with me, and I believe you will come to share my feelings upon seeing his work: It's from the heart.

Michael M. Duprez
Duprez Financial
Myrtle Beach, SC

Ed, a lot of water has flowed under the Toe River Bridge since we met in the eighth grade. We had a blast in the high school years, dating the girls and playing football. Ah, football. You the center and me the punter, I know you remember the time you almost got me killed with the snap that bounced three times despite what you say in "One Little Mistake." I guess it depends on who is telling the story.

We survived the wild years of youth, Washington, DC, and working for the FBI. Thanks to God's work in our lives, we have lived to see our children, grandchildren, and me, my great-grandchildren. Not many people can say they have a friendship that has lasted over 65 years, but we can. I thank God for you and wish His continued blessings on you, my dear friend.

Larry Boyd
Lifetime Friend

I am grateful for the many blessings in my life and the opportunity to work with some of the most amazing people. One of those special people is Ed. Biddix. We worked together in Nashville, Tennessee, and built a strong working and personal relationship. In Ed's book, he will share many of his insights and lessons on life. I know you will enjoy the writings you are about to read.

Robert Ciminelli
Retired Vice President
American Airlines.

I first met my friend, Ed Biddix, when he joined Third Baptist Church (3BC), Murfreesboro, Tennessee, in the spring of 2004, where I served as Director of Missions and Evangelism. Ed felt called into our missions' program and made several trips with our Disaster Relief Team to New Orleans following Hurricane Katrina. In the years that followed, Ed participated in many mission efforts, both evangelical and disaster relief. After my departure from 3BC, Ed led the Disaster Relief Team for about three years. Ed understands the need to "pray, give, and go, putting boots on the ground to honor God and help others. I am honored to call Ed, my friend, and fellow participant in God's Kingdom Work.

Larry Beard
Retired, Pastor

If you ask me, who is Edwin T. Biddix? I would respond, he is family. Growing up, I called him "Skipper," and today, I call him "Skip." We grew up in a quiet valley between mountains known as the "holler" in rural North Carolina. He began sharing his writings with me several years ago, and I found them to be a compelling read. He uses personal stories from his life in heart-rending and comical true tales to inform and share. You will be drawn to the everyday, relaxed, and friendly manner in which he writes. Sit back, relax, grab your favorite drink, and enjoy his book.

Rosalie Lowery-Abell, Retired
Federal Agent, U.S. Government

The author of this book, Edwin T. Biddix, has always been known to me simply as Pa. He is my grandfather. Pa has always motivated and helped me to grow into the best person I can be. He has been a part of my life since birth. Some of my fondest memories are the many things we have done together. I played a lot of baseball as I grew up, and Pa would play catch, take me to the batting cages, come to my games, and do all he could to help me improve. We went to the Tennessee Titans games when I was younger, and often I would ride on his or my dad's shoulders on the long walk to the stadium.

Pa has always been there for me, and I have benefited greatly from his wisdom and advice in all areas of my life. It has been my pleasure to experience some of what you are about to read in this book. Pa's writings are honest, thought-provoking, contain wisdom, humor, and always from his heart. No matter how many books ET Biddix writes or sells, he will always be Pa to me.

Aaron Biddix
Grandson

A Note from the Author

The motivation to write this book came from several sources and in different ways. Nights when sleep eluded me, and old memories, faces, and nostalgia ran through my mind, and would not go away until I wrote it down.

I am well into my seventies and feeling my mortality. Putting pen to paper is my way to thank those who influenced, mentored, loved, and helped me along the way. Telling their stories explains their impact on my life. Perhaps you, too, will gain a better appreciation for the people that shaped your life. Many topics are in my writings, such as the need for forgiveness in "A Follower That Fails." Interesting people I have met in "Ali." Finding true love in "An Encounter That Lasted a Lifetime," and one of my many embarrassing moments in "Finger-Lickin' Good." The poem "An Angel in Sam's Club" is thought provoking, poignant, and beautiful.

I hope these stories will help if you are struggling and bring a smile to your troubled face. There is someone or some event you can identify with and say, "yeah, I can relate to that person, place, or thing."

My faith played a large part in writing this book. God blessed me with a mind for remembering in detail. I began keeping journals of my writings and poems years ago, as well as a list of the people and events to share with others someday.

This book is truly a labor of love. It is not a work of fiction, and I cannot stress that enough. The people are genuine and very dear to me. The names are real, though only first names in some cases. My opinions and impressions are my interpretation of situations, and I give credit if I quoted someone or used another research source.

If you are looking for deep meaning, book club discussion poetry, this book is not for you. My writings tell a story or illustrate a truth, with a dash of opinion and humor thrown in.

The Bible says, "Life is like a vapor; it appears, and it is gone." While my wisp of smoke is fading, it's not extinguished yet. God has been good to me. I remember the past with pride, live today to the fullest, always looking forward to what tomorrow brings.

So, my final reason for my writing would be one of hope. I hope that when reading the pages, you are led to The One who is the Source of all Hope.

I will close with a line often repeated in several of my writings. I look forward to the time when we all sit together and feast around God's Table. I hope you do too.

God bless you and enjoy the book.

CHAPTER 1

Y'all Eat Yet, Come on In, Eat and Talk a Spell

Growing up in the mountains, food, and family time were so important. Folks ate in each other's homes all the time, and conversation was plentiful. Church dinners on the ground, family reunions, community projects, and the local store always found neighbors eating and talking. Everyone's welcome, so come on in!

Mountain Talk

I am a proud son of the Blue Ridge Mountains in Western NC.
A place of rare beauty, and some of the best people in our Country.

The language is unique to the region, and sometimes can be confusing.
It's been described as shortcut, lazy, slang, made up, depending on the word one is using.

To me, it is beautiful, and in this writing, I will attempt to explain
Some of the meaning and flavor of the words that still today remain.

Over "yonder" is a measure of distance, you will hear folks say.
But yonder can be across the yard or a hundred miles away.

A "toe sack" is actually made to carry livestock feed,
But the term is used for a big sack that carries anything you might need.

Now don't confuse a toe sack with a "poke," that comes from the store.
A "poke" comes in all sizes of paper, holding groceries, candy, clothes, and more.

"Airish" means it's pretty cool outside, so dress right.
A "skift" means a light covering of snow fell in the night.

Most people know that folks in the South say y'all.
Mountain people do too, but they also say "you'ens "with a Southern drawl.

A "booger" is not what you think. A "booger" is any kind of ghost.
A "branch" is not a limb off of a tree. It's a creek, just not big as most.

A "wish book" is a long-awaited catalog that comes in the mail.
A "good for nothing" will usually wind up in jail.

A church is the "meeting house" where people go to pray.
"I ain't seen you in a coons age" is said to someone that's been away.

"Si-gogglin" means off-center, out of balance, something is just not right.
"Was you born in a barn" means you didn't shut the door right.

Up in the "holler" is where you live, not something you yell out loud.
And "moonshine" is a drink, not a light, best consumed by yourself and not in a crowd.

I could go on and on about the beautiful language of the mountains from which I came.
I'm proud to be one of them, thankful I was raised there, and return whenever I can!

Little Switzerland Store

Little Switzerland is a community in Mitchell County, NC, located in the western part of the state.
Named for its location in the Blue Ridge Mountains. My family lived there, and I grew up in that beautiful place.

In the heart of the community sits Little Switzerland Store, but it's a far cry from what it used to be.
It's one of many, antiques and books, souvenirs and gallerias, mostly what tourists want to see.

The Post Office is still there, and that's about the only place I become aware of how it used to feel.
You see, back in the day when I was growing up, the store was owned by the Postmaster, Mr. Pete Deal.

I remember, as a small boy, Dad would take me there in the winter when it was cold.
Several older men would be spittin' and whittling, working on the world's problems around the stove.

Pete would always be there, either in the post office or the store.
Cigar firmly in his mouth, but only half or a stub, no more.

His only clerk, Frank, would fix you a sandwich, with tobacco juice dribbling drool down his chin.
His signature line when you got what you came for was, "thanks, and call again."

I remember Mama saying that while Dad was in the War, she or Grandpa would walk the two miles,
Up to Little Switzerland Store to get groceries they needed, even though it took quite a while.

Pete was very accommodating, carrying people on the books when they couldn't pay.
Honest mountain folks, he later told me, he lost very little money to anyone that way.

The store was the hub of the community during the War and until I was grown.
I went there many times with Dad, often when I got older, walking there on my own.

Geneva Hall was just up the road where square dances were held on Saturday night.
I shuffled my feet there a time or two, and occasionally, some drunk would start a fight.

In my teenage years, I worked a number of times for Pete Deal around his home, but never in the store.
He was a good, fair man to work for, paid a sufficient wage, sometimes giving me a little more.

He always supported our football team and was at the games when he could get away.
I know because he always commented on the team and how Johnny and I had played.

Pete is gone now, as are all the old-timers that used to visit and sit a spell at the store.
Dad, Uncle Slim, Gus Washburn, Clay Mcgee, Frank, more McKinney's than I can count, and many more.

I usually try to stop by the Little Switzerland Store each time I return to the Mountains, but of course, it's not the same.
But if I pause, catch a quiet moment and close my eyes, as the wind blows through the pines, long-ago memories and voices from the past will whisper to me again.

How Do You Want Your Eggs??

What makes one remember a phrase, something said by someone a long time ago?
Something insignificant, not what really helps you or something you need to know.

Such was the case when I heard a man say in a cafe in Wilkesboro, NC, in 1959.
I was working with my dad on a road job and living in a boarding house at the time.

How do you want your eggs? I heard the harried waitress ask a man at the table next to mine.
His answer was simple and to the point, as he said, "With a few kind words, that will do just fine."

There is a lesson to be learned in the simple phrase of this lonely man.
Be kind and friendly. There are a lot of sad people wherever you go in this land.

Spit and Whittle Club

They used to be found in small-town America, probably sitting on benches around the Courthouse Square.
Farmers, retired businessmen, old-timers from all walks of life were found there,

And they solved the perplexing problems of the day.
As these wise men talked, spit, and whittled their life away.

They discussed politics, religion, sports, the weather, local gossip, local events, and things that happened far away.
Why it's been said someone knew everything, and if a question went unanswered, he just wasn't there that day.

In winter they moved inside if they could, but most went to the local old country store,
Where they sat around the stove, whittled and spit, and told them old lies once more.

A lot of farming was done around that stove as they told how many acres they were going to plow.
But if you drove by their place come spring, it all didn't seem to materialize as they planned on somehow.

New concrete patios and sidewalks at the courthouse drove out the Spit and Whittle Club.
Seven Elevens replace their dwellings for the winter as the old country stores went away.

You can still find these men, always full of knowledge, but now they sit in Hardees, McDonald's, Shoney's, or some other breakfast store.
They are still brimming with wisdom, and anxious to share, they just can't whittle and spit on the floor anymore.

Dedicated to old men of wisdom everywhere.

Coffee

I know people that appear grouchy and mean in the morning when they get up.
Surly, uncaring, stumbling around like a drunken sailor until they get that first cup.

Then, right before your eyes, an amazing transformation begins.
They become all smiley and almost human, wanting to be your friend.

What causes this transformation that takes place there in front of you??
Why it's a simple cup of coffee, that magical, back to life, brew.

But be warned if anything goes wrong in the process they are as likely as not,
To throw whatever is handy, and you might have to duck when they throw the pot.

People marvel when I tell them that in my life, I haven't drunk ten cups of coffee. They think it's a joke.
I tell them nope, no joke but not to worry. I get my caffeine through another source-Diet Coke.

I don't want you to think I'm self-righteous, so if you look you can plainly see,
If I'm denied my Diet Coke, then the first few verses of this little story also apply to me.

Mountain Cookin'

Mountain cookin' raises your blood pressure and takes that grease straight to your heart.
Will send you running to the bathroom, gives you gas, and makes you fart.

There is no way most of it will ever pass the cholesterol test.
But you eat a big plate of pinto beans, then tofu and tell me which is best.

Let's start with breakfast, the most important meal of the day.
Gimme three (aig's), eggs, bacon and sausage, pancakes, and by the way,

Let me have about three of them biscuits and pass that gravy bowl.
Let me try all three of them jellies and a couple of cinnamon rolls.

I think I will pass on the Krispy Kreme donuts and the fruit salad today.
On second thought, bag me some up to eat as a snack along the way.

The Country Store on Grassy Creek

It didn't look like much from the outside, a couple of aging gas pumps, a Purina sign, and a screen door.
But to us folks that lived out in the country, the Store at Grassy Creek was so much more

It was a place to pick up a few things you needed, sit and talk a spell with folks you know.
It had a big old wood stove in one end, and in the winter, I've seen the fire so hot that the potbelly would glow.

The owner, Charlie, had a counter where you could get a cold cut sandwich made to order.
Meat, mayonnaise, or mustard was only twenty cents. If you wanted cheese, it was a quarter.

The bologna, lunch meat, and cheese he sliced off a stalk or block, so thick it would make your mouth water.
Why I've bought two sandwiches, a Moon Pie, and a cold drink and got change back out of a dollar.

Crops were raised around that stove and oh, the hunting tales that were told, and who had been caught making booze.
Which one had the best coon dogs, the fattest cattle, who got divorced, and how many games the football team would lose

But let a stranger come through the door, and conversation would come to a halt or a murmur as they suspiciously eyed the one who came in.
If someone knew him or her, it was ok. Otherwise, they waited until the newcomer left before they started talking again.

Charlie oversaw everything with a welcoming nod, a friendly smile, and taking care of one and all.
I've bought my lunch there many times and joined the conversation when I was playing football.

Long before anyone ever heard of credit cards, Charlie kept a record of charges until one could pay.
An invaluable service to a lot of folks, especially teenagers like me back in the day.

The Grassy Creek Country Store is gone now, replaced by a Walmart just down the road and up on the hill.
Impersonal, uncaring, cash-driven, never really caring for their customer's needs. Never did. Never will.

I only get back to where the old store stood, oh maybe once or twice a year. But I pause a bit as I drive by, and if I listen carefully, I can almost hear,

The ding of the gas pumps, hear Daddy, Uncle Slim, Bobby, and other old-timers as they sit around the stove and solve the problems of the day.
Sadly though, it's just a childhood memory, forever in my mind. Another time, another place, and another piece of Americana gone away.

Mom and Pop Stores

Born in 1943, I have enjoyed my life to the fullest. I know of no other era that so much change has taken place.
I'm not one that longs for "the good old days" although, sometimes I wish we could slow down the pace.

One thing, however, that is fast disappearing, and I am afraid we will soon not see anymore,
Is the locally owned market, shop, or local business, commonly known as The Mom and Pop stores.

These friendly places have been the backbone of many towns and hamlets throughout our land.
That folks have abandoned them now is a shame, and hard for them to understand.

However, times change and, life goes on, big box stores and online shopping puts loyalty to the test.
People, including me, want variety, convenience, lower prices, and all the rest.

We put up with crowds, poor service, giving our money to big corporations that do not care
Many times, it was our tax money and other incentives that enticed these companies to come here.

I often think of the small businesses where I would go and how it used to be.
Friendly people, excellent service, I always felt welcome. I knew them, and they knew me.

We are fast losing a part of Americana as we see these Mom and Pops close their doors.
Progress, they say. Changing times, they say. Still, it's sad that not many are around anymore.

So, it's Target, Walmart, and Amazon. We are not going back to shopping as we did in 1964.
But every now and then, if you can find one, patronize a friendly Mom and Pop store.

Birthdays at Our House

As with everything else she does, my wife goes out of her way,
And adds an extraordinary twist to each of our birthdays.

She asks about two weeks in advance what we would like to eat.
And she gets great enjoyment out of preparing our favorite treats.

For son, Tommy, the food is simple when it comes to what she makes:
Pinto beans, onions and greens, potatoes, corn, and super delicious chocolate cake.

Bobby is a bit different, saying he doesn't care.
But seems mighty pleased when juicy, beefy hamburgers and moist, chewy, homemade cookies are there.

A breakfast fare suits Aaron, and with country cured ham, he is especially pleased.
Oh, and he would probably be looking for some creamy and oh-delicious macaroni and cheese.

Me? Oh, I like all the above, everything passes my test.
But if I had to choose one, I guess I like fresh, country vegetables best.

But each year brings a problem that I have to work through.
Because, even though she never looks any older, Margaret has a birthday too.

As her birthday gets close, the fun starts as the family teases and gives me that look.
Asking, joking, and wondering, what do you think this year, "Pa's going to cook?"

Now you may think that's a valid question, but it's not, and I'll tell you why.
I don't know the first thing about cooking. Don't want to know. Don't want to try.

So, I do what any thoughtful, caring husband would do.
Load up on Kentucky Fried Chicken, Chick-fil-A, and barbecue.

After a few years, choices are getting slim, and I'm running out of places to go.
Looks like I may have to learn to cook, but will that ever happen——No!!

Still, I thank my wife for starting and continuing this birthday tradition yearlong.
It's a means of loving, caring for each other, and helps keep our family strong.

Walnut Cake

Christmas time growing up in the Mountains was a grand time for this young boy.
And a lot of it had to do with the delicious homemade goodies Mama made for us to enjoy.

I remember how much work it took, and all the time she had to take,
But for her, a labor of love to bake and give away her famous flavorful Walnut Cakes.

You see, there in the Mountains, black walnut trees were all about.
So, Mama gathered the walnuts, let them dry, and then crack them out.

I have seen a gallon jar full of the richest black walnuts you would ever see.
I helped her sometimes, but the cracking was much to slow for me.

She usually baked about ten two-layer cakes to give away.
And if I close my eyes, I can still smell the aroma that filled the house that day.

You see she, baked those walnuts in the cakes, but that was not all she would do.
She spread sweet, warm, caramel icing over the cakes and placed black walnuts all over it too.

I don't know how much time she spent on those cakes before she got them all done.
But you could see the joy that it brought her as she gave them away to relatives one by one.

While I was home, I took the cakes for granted because they were always there.
After we got married and returned home for Christmas, there was always one for us to share.

There are a lot of memories from the Blue Ridge Mountains Margaret, and I continue to take.
Memories of family, mountain cooking, and Mamas one of a kind Walnut Cake.

CHAPTER 2

Mountains and Relatives – Forever With Us

In the Blue Ridge Mountains, where I grew up, after the Almighty, family was next in importance. In this chapter, you will meet a few relatives of mine. Many of them appear in later writings, so I hope you will enjoy getting to know them now. And you might find one or two, just like someone in your family!

Family Tree

I started research one time on my family tree.
I guess I wanted to learn about those that preceded me.

It wasn't long before my research turned grim.
I found some mighty strange birds sitting on them limbs.

So, I gave up, stopped the research, trashed the papers, let it go.
I found out that there were things that I just did not want to know.

The Blue Ridge Mountains

While growing up in the mountains, I never could see,
The beautiful world God had created all around me.

Times were hard. The winters were rough,
Beans, potatoes, corn, beans again, but we all had enough.

My family was great, we went to church and worked hard,
I had plenty of cousins that I played with in the yard.

As I began to grow older, my mind would often stray,
Beyond the mountains to places far away.

I married my sweetheart and soon began to see,
Her thoughts ranged far beyond the mountains, same as me.

So the day we got married we moved away,
All we owned in the world packed in a 1952 Chevrolet.

Now sixty years later we have lived in a lot of places,
Flown all over the world, explored, met friendly faces.

We've been back to the mountains more times than we can name,
To visit those we love, but it's never been the same.

Close family have passed away, only cousins survive,
The Blue Ridge, however, still stands majestic and alive.

So I wonder sometimes what would have happened had we stayed,
Would we have been happy the way our life would be played?

We have talked of this often, and we have no regrets.
Life has been wonderful for both of us and yet…

We sometimes get to thinking of the mountains and our early days,
When life seemed simple in so many ways.

And it is very comforting each time we return,
To the place of our birth, and one thing we've learned,

Very few things in life stay the same,
But the mountains are there, and in our hearts, they remain.

Faye Lowery Biddix (My Mother)

My Mother is in many of my writings, and now I am writing solely about her.
I guess it's because she was a complicated person, hard to put in perspective, as it were.

Upfront, I will say I really loved her, she was my Mother after all.
But she often had a way of driving those who loved her up a wall.

She was the youngest of nine children, two brothers, and six sisters born in the mountains of Western NC.
It was a hardscrabble life, the Great Depression, living on a mountain farm, life was as hard as it could be.

Being the youngest probably made Grandpa Lowery spoil her and make her his favorite child.
That plus having fiery red hair, a quick temper, and mood swings probably explained why she seldom smiled.

She graduated high school in Spruce Pine, worked in a hosiery mill before she met and married my dad.
She enjoyed reading, poetry, and her family, especially staying close and visiting all the sisters she had.

She always took good care of my sister and me as we grew up, urging us and supporting us in school.
She went when she could to our activities, taught us right from wrong, whipped us when we acted a fool.

My little brother, William Douglas, died right about the time he was three months old.
I don't think Mama ever got over that, and for years his death weighed on her and took its toll.

She was a very religious person, taught the young people in Sunday School. Read her Bible daily, helped others when she could, and lived mostly by the Golden Rule.

Still, she had that temper, and mood swings made her hard to please, blowing cold and hot.
I think for the above reasons, my dad, who ran a bulldozer, worked away from home a lot.

Mama embraced all her sisters, always going to see them, worrying about them and their families.
Sometimes it seemed, and I may be wrong, that they came before Daddy, Polly, and me.

One of the hardest things that I had to deal with was the fact that she never fully accepted Margaret as my wife.
Margaret was gracious to her; however, she never came around, but a little, and that was at the end of her life.

She loved my sons, Tommy and Bobby, and they enjoyed the weeks in the summer spent with her and Dad at their home.
Unfortunately, Dad passed away at an early age, 64, and Mama for the first time in her life, except when Polly was there, was alone.

I believe she liked it that way. Thinking back now as best I can recall, I don't think that she ever spent many happy days at all.

Mama always seemed to be a negative person, usually seeing the bad and never the good.
She did not make friends easily, tended to push people away, and was generally misunderstood.

Still, she was a hard worker and took loving care of Grandpa and Grandma Lowery until they died.
She did the same with Daddy, in her own, sometimes strange way, she loved us all down deep inside.

As I said before, she had a hard life, blind her last ten years, and struggled in a lot of ways none of us will ever understand.
Still, she was my Mother, and I loved her. Her pain and heartache are gone now, and one day soon, I will see her in that beautiful Heavenly Land.

Rest in Peace, Mama

Helen and Burl

Some things belong together, such as wedding and ring, love and marriage, boy and girl.
So, it is and was with two of the most exceptional people I have ever known in my lifetime, Helen and Burl.

Helen and Burl Willis, my in-laws, I knew for the better part of my life.
I was around eighteen when I started dating, Margaret, one of their five daughters, who later became my wife.

I can still remember going to pick up Margaret, Helen's warm welcome, Burl's suspicious stare.
I guess he knew I was the one that would someday take his beloved daughter away from there.

But he warmed up to me over the years, and eventually, he saw,
How much I loved Margaret, and I became his devoted son-in-law.

It wasn't long, even while we were dating that I felt as welcome as anyone could be.
And I feel so fortunate today for the tremendous love and acceptance of a second family.

Married for over sixty years, they raised six children on their small farm on Rabbit Hop Road
Burl farmed, worked on the railroad, and in a factory, while Helen stayed home and carried that heavy load.

One thing they always had was an enormous garden, the pride of the neighborhood.
Beans, potatoes, onions, tomatoes, okra, squash, and everything else that was good.

Burl loved to raise cattle, and he always had several head.
Spent hours working the hay so, in the winter, they could be fed.

Helen planted, hoed, and harvested the garden, then canned or froze most everything she grew.
And whoever came to see them, she gave some of that bountiful garden, when their visit was through.

They were the most welcoming, loving, and friendly people you would ever want to meet or see.
I believe Margaret and I could have sent friends or strangers to them, and they would be treated like family.

When Helen and Burl found out we sent them, they would be welcomed and given a place to stay,
And upon leaving, they would have a box of canned food to send them on their way.

Margaret and I often talked about all they had to do, how hard they had to work, every day.
No time for vacations or recreation, genuinely enjoying each other, family, and the simple pleasures that came their way.

Helen and Burl have passed on. The farm divided up, the house has been sold. We drive by there, and it's not the same. But we have precious memories that never grow old.

And my thoughts of the past center around Helen and Burl, and I always think of them as one.
My second parents, two of the finest, toughest of the tough, mountain people that I have ever known.

Rest in Peace. God Bless You Both

Johnny Simmons

One of my regrets in life, and believe me I have more than a few,
So, telling people close to me how I feel about them is hard for me to do.

Such is the case with my first cousin, Johnny Simmons, a year younger than me.
We grew up together in the beautiful Blue Ridge Mountains, near Little Switzerland, NC.

We lived about three football fields apart, in a holler, on a gravel road.
The first to get on the school bus in the morning, the last to unload.

Johnny had two sisters, me a sister, and a little brother that passed away.
I considered Johnny the brother I never had and still do today.

Our mothers were sisters; therefore, we were back and forth between houses, playing to our heart's content.
Then we would get in a fight, and our mamas would get together and separate us for a bit.

We roamed all over those mountains together, hunting, fishing, and camping out.
Back then, wildlife was mainly squirrels, possums, rabbits, raccoons, grouse, and trout.

I helped his dad, Uncle Slim, and him build houses in the summer and any other time that I could.
Uncle Slim was a hard worker, expected the same, always treated me fairly and good.

Johnny and I played on the football team and after work no matter how late,
We would run to get in playing shape for Coach Norton's opening practice date.

After high school in a strange twist of fate, Johnny worked for a time with my dad, Tommy, building roads.
Operating heavy equipment pans, that carried weighted loads.

Our paths took separate directions, and to tell them all would take too long to do.
However, we traveled to Wisconsin together to work for Del Monte, and that alone would take a chapter or two.

Suffice it to say we went different ways, Johnny, to college at East Tennessee State University, ETSU.
Me to Appalachian for a year, then to the FBI, and American Airlines until my career was through.

Johnny taught school for a while, but what he loved called and he went to work at what he did best,
Building quality homes in Mitchell County for local folks, flatlanders (Florida people), and the rest.

Both of us married girls from high school, me, Margaret, Johnny, JoAnn.
Marriages, I believe, were all part of the Makers plan.

We kept in touch with cards, Christmas presents, and visits whenever that could be.
Over the years, that's been quite often as we came back to see our families from Tennessee.

When my sister, Polly, passed away, Johnny helped in a multitude of ways.
Getting a lawyer, loaning his truck, JoAnn selling the house, a sale that took many, many days.

Then came that day last December, the phone call when he told us JoAnn had passed away.
We prayed and packed and drove to North Carolina for the funeral the next day.

With true lifetime friends, few words are spoken in times of sickness, death, and stress.
One's presence, a hand on the shoulder, the look in the eyes says it best.

You know we are blessed indeed to have a friendship that has lasted these many years.
From toddler to high school, adult to old age, through laughter, good times, heartache, and tears.

Here's to you, my cousin and lifetime friend.
May you enjoy good health and happiness until your day's end.

And one day soon with no heartache or pain we will be able,
To sit down and feast forever around God's table.

Pauline Susan Biddix (My Sister)

The most complex member of my family to write about,
Is my sister "Polly" and of this I have not one bit of doubt.

First, let me say I loved her, and at age fifty-nine, she left us before her time.
She left me, my family, cousins, and countless friends, behind.

Polly had a winning personality that would make you forget your troubles, heartache, and strife.
She could walk into a room full of strangers, and when she left, they felt like they had known her all their lives.

She was a hard worker, working all her life at this job and that.
Loved animals and ALWAYS had a dog and an occasional cat.

Still, there were many sides to my sister that a lot of folks did not see.
She was moody; her emotions would change unpredictably, and often, she could be a bit of a mystery.

She never married, lived mostly alone, had few boyfriends one could name.
She drank a bit, had a terrible temper, and at times could be very profane.

We never were close as brother and sister, probably because of the nine years difference in age.
I was the older brother, and when we got grown, we never seemed to be on the same page.

Polly never planned anything. She lived hour by hour, day by day.
This made for a carefree life, but at some time, a price one must pay.

And that lifestyle often led to debt, and my sister would often come to me for a loan.
Payback never came, so I finally just gave her the money, told her to forget about it and go on.

She loved to fish, was great with our two young sons when they visited there.
Polly took good care of Mama, with my financial help, and saw she got the best of care.

She was the historian of the family, always knew who was related to who.
I catch myself now, almost picking up the phone to call her about someone I knew.

So, Rest in Peace, my sister, in the land where all is fresh and clean.
Know that I love you and will soon be coming to see you again.

Aunt Nell

On my mother's side of the family, I had six aunts, all of whom are deceased now.
I loved them all, but Aunt Nell Simmons was always my favorite somehow.

I guess it was because we lived close together in the "holler" where Dale road came to an end.
Three families, all related, lived there: my family, Cousin Bobby and Esther, Aunt Nell and Uncle Slim.

My sister Polly and I, Nell Edith and Rosalie, Johnny and Becky, were her "young'uns" as I recall.
She was always glad when we came to see her, loved us, fed us, kind of a second mother to us all.

She was larger in stature than her mother, Grandma Lowery, but had her mannerisms and loving heart.
And if you went by facial expression and her movements, you could not have told them apart.

Aunt Nell was the only one of the nine Lowery children not to finish school with her class.
A situation in the family required her to take care of some sick folks, so I think the tenth grade was her last.

While she never said a lot, she always had a twinkle in her eyes.
And oh, my goodness! She could cook, especially cakes and pies.

There was never a time, when playing with my cousin Johnny, and I did that a lot,
When she didn't feed me supper, I smelled cooking in the pots.

She knew mountain medicine, the herbs, the plants, all the remedies of the old ways.
One time she took a painful boil off my shoulder in only two days.

I had seen the doctor, he gave me some pills and said come back in a day or two.
Mama said, go see your Aunt Nell. She more than likely will know what to do.

I did, and she cut a piece of fatback, taped a plastic shield over it so I could put on my football shoulder pads.
Told me to come back the next morning, but have Mama put a fresh piece of meat on it before I went to bed.

The next morning I went back, and she took a pair of tweezers and pulled a three-inch large mass out, and immediately, the pain went away.
The thing was hideous looking, like a small white stringy carrot I can still see in my mind to this day.

That was my Aunt Nell, a true Mountain Lady, gentle, yet strong, and kind to all that she met.
She would love them, doctor them, if needed, and feed them pie or cake they would never forget.

She's just one of the people that make me proud of my heritage, where I grew up, the land of my birth.
My Aunt Nell, I love her and think of her often. Just one of many Mountain people of my youth. The greatest people on earth.

Esther, A True Lady

I was born in March of 1943 with World War Two still going on.
I was too young to remember much, except when our loved ones came home.

My first cousin, Bobby Lowery, came home with a young bride that caused quite a fuss.
I didn't know what they were talking about when I heard "she doesn't look like us."

Now I need to pause right here and tell you that mountain folks are the best in the land,
It's just that they warm up slowly to people that look different or those they don't understand.

And Esther Delucca Lowery was from Puerto Rico, brown eyes, dark complexion, and hair as black as coal.
Relatives said she didn't look like she was from these parts or fit the mountain woman mold.

I can't remember when I first saw her, and I'm sure I was well past three.
I didn't see what the commotion was about; Esther looked all right to me.

Moving with charm and grace, she made her way in the new life and home she had found.
And ever so slowly, the wives, sisters, and grown-up cousins began to warm up to her and come around.

See, here's the thing. Sometimes people react differently and can seem cold as ice.
Esther, being the lady she was, overcame the cold shoulder treatment by merely being nice.

Soon she was part of a big mountain family, loved, and respected by all.
My favorite memory is seeing her laughing and talking to Grandpa at our reunions in the fall.

In cold or rainy weather, my sister, Polly, and I often waited on the school bus in her home.
We were always welcome, and she never complained about mud tracks from the shoes we had on.

Bobby and Esther's daughters, Nell Edith and Rosalie, cousins, Johnny, Becky, and Polly and me,
Grew up together in that mountain holler, playing and going to school together, happy as we could be.

Time passes so fast, one minute you are a kid, you turn around, and you are grown.
What a shame we don't tell people how much they mean to us before they are gone.

I often think of Esther, the difficulties and problems she faced while maintaining her dignity.
And try to apply her philosophy to those that I encounter that don't look like you and me.

No matter people's occupation, skin color or from what part of the world they came,
We are all God's children, and He loves us all the same.

I think if Esther were here, she would flash a smile, probably once or twice,
And say in her unique way of speaking, love God and others, and please be nice.

Aunt Duskey

My mother, Faye, had six sisters, very different from each other, so to speak.
Strong mountain women, all, but only one stood out as being unique.

Rhoady Lo Duskey was her name, and that name was not all that stood out.
Aunt Duskey walked to the beat of a different drum, not worried what others thought about.

She was a bit gaudy, a little too much makeup, kind of spacey, and word was she saw several different men.
And she never talked much about her gentlemen callers and was secretive about where she had been.

But she was always kind to me when she came to visit Grandpa, usually bringing me some little toy.
Toys were scarce then, so you tend to remember with fondness those who gave you some as a boy.

I know at Christmas, Polly and I could always count on something under the tree from her,
And we always got her lipstick, perfume, or makeup, which is what she preferred.

I remember when I started shaving, she gave me Clubman Shaving Lotion, a hard to find brand.
It was a great fragrance, and try as I might, I have never been able to find those small green bottles again.

In my early teenage years, Mama never had any problem with letting me go,
On a different school bus to spend the night with Aunt Duskey every few weeks or so.

Now I had an ulterior motive as I asked to spend the night from time to time. I would sneak off to meet a couple of girls down by the creek after Aunt Duskey went to bed at nine.

This went on for a long time, this rendezvous in the woods after night fell. And as far as I know, Aunt Duskey didn't catch on, and the two girls nor I never did tell.

When I got my driver's license, I would often drive her to get her groceries in Spruce Pine.
She would always hand me a dollar, but knowing her situation, I refused most of the time.

While I know her sisters loved her; she sure gave them something to talk and gossip about now and then.
Didn't seem to bother Aunt Duskey though, she carried on just like she had always been.

I loved her also, but could not attend her funeral when she died because of living so far away.
She was a part of my life growing up, and I shed a tear when I think of her today.

We need to be aware of those God puts in our path, those just a bit different, doing what others won't or can't.
My life is much richer, and my outlook is brighter. I am a more tolerant person, for knowing and loving this precious Aunt.

Bobby and Ted

I had many first cousins as I grew up, and on Sunday, a lot of folks, cousins, and others had to be fed.
But two of the older ones, brothers, lived there year-round, and their names were Bobby and Ted.

They lived with Grandpa and Grandma Lowery as they grew up and played. Just how and why they lived there, I'm not sure, but that's a story for another day.

I know they loved Grandpa, and he returned that love and treated them as his sons.
They reciprocated by working on the mountain farm side by side with Grandpa until the work was done.

Bobby went into the Marines in World War II. I guess Ted was too young.
Mama said every time she wrote my dad a letter; she wrote Bobby one.

Dad and Bobby were spared in the war, and Bobby came home with Esther, his beautiful new bride.
Bobby and my dad built new houses, sturdy homes that they lived in until they died.

Ted married Sylvia, tried several jobs before becoming an insurance agent in Marion, NC.
Bobby went to work for the American Thread Plant at that time, a brand-new company.

Most of my memories of these two first cousins began when Grandpa and Grandma came to live with us in 1949.
Few days passed that one of them was not at our house, helping out all the time.

Grandma died just before Christmas in 1952 from cancer and other things.
We had been living in Marion, but we moved back to Little Switzerland in the Spring.

With Daddy working away from home, Ted in Marion, Bobby, helped out the most.
He was there nearly every day, doing whatever needed doing, and we became very close.

We gardened, cut wood, fenced, planted trees, made repairs, did whatever had to be done.
I was in shape, playing football, and could keep up with Bobby, but he was one strong son of a gun.

We both loved Grandpa and always did what we could,
To keep him comfortable, and that meant getting lots of wood.

No chainsaws then. Crosscut saws, wedges, and axes were the order of the day. One day, while we were sawing my cousin gave me the highest compliment he had to pay.

A man of few words, he said, "Skip, you are a very good sawyer," the exact words he had to say.
I still remember the exact spot we were when he told me that on a Saturday.

Bobby Lowery was a complicated man. Talk flowed smoothly at times, other times quiet as he could be.
He would sometimes call me "Skidwin," but I didn't care. He loved Grandpa, and that made him all right with me.

As far as I recall, we never had a crossword during all the work we had to do. However, he is one of about eight men I've known that would not blink if they had to shoot you.

I never knew Ted as well as Bobby, but he came to see Grandpa, usually on the weekend days.
He would come to football practice some and came to several games to watch me play.

Mama thought the world of both, but Bobby was her special one,
Saying, after Grandpa got sick, if not for his help, she doesn't know what she would have done.

As I finish this journey down memory lane, suddenly it begins to dawn,
That everyone except Sylvia and me has passed on.

And so, it goes. Life moves on with or without us. I am thankful to still be here, but yet,
I am grateful for individuals that helped shape me, folks I will never forget.

I look forward to the day when we will see those we love that have gone on before.
And rejoice with our Savior, family, and friends that cared for us, forevermore.

William Douglas Biddix (My Little Brother)

My little brother that I never got to know,
I was only three years old when you had to go.

Living just three months, you were the only brother I ever had.
My only memory of you is standing at your grave, feeling sad.

I know Mama and Daddy never got over losing you, and until their death mourned you so.
I was too young to miss you then; however, through the years, I often think of you, though.

I think of what it may have been like to have a younger brother,
Someone to play with and later help take care of Dad and Mother.

What might have been your personality, or some of the things that you would want to do?
Perhaps we'd have played on the high school football team together, me and you?

I've often wondered why God took you at such an early age to be with Him.
However, He knew what was best for you, saw your future, and what might have been.

But if one believes the Bible, Jesus Words and has faith as I do,
It won't be long as I walk toward my sunset until I will be seeing you.

Rest in Peace, Little Brother

CHAPTER 3

My Dad, My Hero

Tommy Biddix, my Dad, left home at age thirteen to escape an abusive father. Finishing only the eighth grade, he was one of the most educated men I have ever known. Mother said the first year they were married was his first Christmas to celebrate, and after that, he was like a kid every year. A road builder, he was second to none, an exceptional bulldozer operator. He knew roadwork, and engineers often sought his advice. A Veteran of World War Two, he served in the European Theater and was in Paris on Victory in Europe Day. A member of The Greatest Generation, Tommy Biddix, died at the young age of sixty-four. He was and will always be my hero.

Daddy, Grandpa, and Christmas

As the season progresses, each year, my mind returns to the Mountains where Christmas for me began.
And I am very thankful that in my formative years, I was blessed to be surrounded by faithful, strong, family men.

There was my Dad, of course, and Grandpa Lowery, I sure can't forget him.
On up the road lived two others I loved, an older cousin Bobby Lowery and my Uncle Slim.

But what I hope to share with you as I write these lines,
Is how two tough old Mountain men became kids at Christmas time.

My Dad, Tommy Biddix, left home at age thirteen to escape beatings and all kinds of strife.
Mama said the first Christmas they were married was the only Christmas he had celebrated in his life.

He had no idea about getting a tree, presents, or the One the day was celebrated for.
But boy did he learn and love it!! Daddy became the biggest kid you ever saw at Christmas after the War.

He always spent too much money, but not just on the family alone.
We always took boxes of food and toys to those less fortunate that lived not far from our home.

I can see him now, always wearing his red socks and enjoying every moment of the Christmas season.
Visiting with relatives down in Marion, and helping get wood or anything else someone needed within reason.

Grandpa and Grandma, on the other hand, always celebrated Christmas, Mama said.
But with nine children in the Blue Ridge, it was often a struggle just to get everyone fed.

Despite hard times though, according to Mama, there was always something in their sock.
Maybe an orange, a few nuts, a handkerchief, and a peppermint stick that was hard as a rock.

So, when times were better, and Grandpa lived with us, it was then he became a kid again.
Presents came from his children and grandchildren, and I would help him open them as he sat and grinned.

You see, Grandpa Lowery had a nervous disorder that made his hands shake. Only bothered him eating and holding small things. Never reading his Bible or holding an ax or rake.

He certainly enjoyed watching Polly and me opening our presents, and I have often said,
That he had been awake and waiting a long time for us to stir and get out of bed.

I always got him a giant stick of peppermint candy, the rock-hard kind.
He would smile and say, Skip, you know what I want every time.

I'm an old man now; I think a lot about the past. Nostalgia, no matter how I fight it, creeps in.
I can close my eyes, hear the rustle of the paper, and see these two tough old Mountain men celebrate again.

And always, always, today if you look hard enough among the presents under our family tree,
Somewhere there is a hard stick of peppermint candy. It's tradition, just like Grandpa would want it to be.

Belts

The other day as I dressed it occurred to me,
How a specific sound can trigger an unpleasant childhood memory.

I thought of the distinct sounds I heard that were soothing and sweet,
Like the gentle rain on a tin roof that put me to sleep.

There is one sound, though, that made me quiver.
And when I think of it today, I still get the shivers.

When I had a whipping coming whatever the circumstance,
I can still hear the crackling swoosh that belt made as it cleared the last loop in Daddy's pants.

Dad and the War

In the prime of his life at the age of thirty-one,
My Dad went off to WWII, leaving my mother and me, his only son.

He was in the Combat Engineers; I heard him once say,
Fighting the Germans across Europe, he ended up in Paris on VE Day.

Many questions I asked him, about battles and where he had been.
He would look at me sadly, I guess, thinking of what he had seen.

Son, he would say, that was a long time ago, and I want to forget,
Besides, you're too young to know about things like that.

The only story about the War I ever heard him say
Was about feeding German prisoners while guarding them one Christmas Day.

Putting some thrown away scraps of food on a garbage can lid,
He pushed it under the fence, and a few prisoners got fed.

My grandpa lived with us, so a lot of cousins and uncles that were in WWII were always about.
But when talk of the War began, I remember my Dad would slowly make his way out.

He never sought any recognition, honors, thanks, or accolades.
Dad would tell you he was not worthy of marching in any Veterans Day Parades.

He did his duty with grace, dignity, and courage, as did most of his generation.
It was him and thousands like him that put it all on the line and saved this nation.

Still, I wish he would have told me more of what he went through,
Places, firepower, Germans, and the people he knew.

If Dad had lived to talk to Tommy, Bobby, and Aaron, his grandsons,
I think he would have been more open than he was about some of the things he had done.

A member of "The Greatest Generation," most of those like him, are now fading away.
And I wonder if young people realize it's because of these heroes we are not speaking German or Japanese today.

Tommy Biddix, my Dad, is gone, and not much of his War experiences did he ever tell.
I loved this quite man, and I salute him. He served this country he loved, and he served it well.

Cutting Wood

When I was growing up in the mountains as a young lad,
Gathering, cutting, and chopping wood were some of the chores I had.

It was something I hated to do; we never seemed to have enough.
And we were always outside getting wood when the weather was rough.

With three stoves in the old frame house, a lot of wood was consumed.
There was the kitchen stove, bedroom where Grandpa slept, and the living room.

I remember days when it was raining or snowing,
Daddy would say get your coat on; we've got to get going.

Off we would go with axes and saws into the woods close by,
And saw, cut, split, and haul until there was no light in the sky.

I guess that's the reason when I got grown and moved away,
I made the vow that I have never broken to this day.

The vow was that I would do the best I could,
To never be in the position to have to cut another stick of wood.

Now don't get me wrong, I'm not too good to do it, I'm not saying that at all.
But I sure appreciate that little round thermostat hanging on the wall.

Honest Work

Dad worked away from home a lot, so it was a treat when he was home, and we would go,
Down off the mountain to Marion, a small town fifteen to twenty miles away or so.

I guess I must have been nine or ten and one Saturday we were in Marion town,
And went into the local Dime store food counter, found a stool and sat down

I don't remember what we ordered, but I do remember the little kid across the way.
He made a big mess out of a banana split, then he and his mother just walked away.

An older black man came with a bucket and mop and began to clean the counter and mop the floor.
I made the mistake of saying, "If I had to do that, I'd quit and not work here anymore."

Daddy spun me around on the stool, and, as only he could do, said these words I will never forget.
"That man is doing honest work, trying to support his family, doing the very best he can, I'll bet."

"Don't you ever look down on anyone no matter their work or what you see. And remember that throughout our lives, someone will be cleaning up after you and me."

Dads words and my background in organized labor today creates a huge place in my heart,
For the waitress, janitor, maid, groundskeeper, and others that do the jobs of which we want no part.

So, leave a generous tip, speak the person's name, ask them how they are doing, and say a kind word or two.
It is so appreciated when you or I acknowledge them, and I know that's what my Dad would want me to do.

Eyes in the Back of His Head

As I grew up in the Blue Ridge Mountains to every church service, we were sure to go.
I headed for the bench in the very back corner; Daddy always sat on the second row.

One thing still bugs me today, remembering that he never turned his head,
He always knew when I was misbehaving, could hear nearly all I had said.

Laughing and talking with friends in church might keep me in stitches,
But once I got home, Daddy would warm up my britches.

What Fair??

Once growing up Dad told me to do a chore,
That my sister, Polly, was supposed to do, but she ignored.

That's not fair, I told Daddy that day.
I'm doing her work while she runs and plays.

The words I then heard my Dad say,
I still use with my sons, Tommy and Bobby, today.

Fair, fair? There is no fair here that I know about.
If there were one, I think I would have found out.

But the fair will be here in the fall, don't you know?
And if we get our work done, we will all try to go.

But as for now, son, let me make one thing clear,
You do what I tell you, cause there ain't no fair here.

Dad and Football

My Dad did not understand sports of any kind at all.
Probably did not know the difference between a tennis ball and a baseball.

So, when I made the high school football team my freshman year and told him I was going to play,
He was not at all impressed and asked me kind of impatiently, how much does it pay?

Now it was most every young man's dream to play for the Blue Devils of Harris High.
And I thought my Dad would be impressed that I made the team on my very first try.

I explained to him that there was no pay; it would require me to practice after school nearly every weekday.
Dad said, okay, although I don't see any sense in it, two things will get your football taken away.

First off, the work you have to do will still be waiting for you when practice is done, and you get home.
Second, and most important, if your grades start to fall, then football will be over and gone.

Well, I abided by his rules, and before I knew it, two years of football and classes had gone by in a flash.
Then one day, Dad surprised me by asking, are you playing or still sitting on the bench?

I'm playing, I told him. I play center and sometimes linebacker when the other teams got the ball.
Daddy looked bewildered and said I don't know what center and linebacker means at all.

Are you planning on coming to a game sometime, I asked, and he said he

might someday.
I told him the center was the first one to touch the ball, and his snap puts the ball in play.

It was a beautiful October Friday night when we traveled down the mountain to play Glen Alpine.
Dad was working as a foreman on a road job in Hickory, about thirty miles away at the time.

It was always a rugged game when we played the Green Wave, and as we ran off the field at halftime,
I saw my Dad, attending his first football game ever, standing behind the rope at the forty-yard line.

I can't describe how it made me feel, and I hardly remember the second half, except that we won the game.
I kept looking over at where Dad was, very emotional that in my senior year, he finally, finally came.

When he arrived home on Saturday evening, I asked him how he enjoyed the game.
It looks like you did good son, he said. Other than that, I didn't understand a dang thing.

Daddy came to one other game, a home game, in Spruce Pine; however, I can't remember the team.
As far as I know, in my four years of playing football, only those two games were attended by him.

But those two games stand out in my memory, vivid as if they happened only yesterday.
And although he didn't say it, I know that tough, time-honored WW2 veteran was proud of his son's play.

I guess that's why I tried to attend every game and event that my two sons and grandson had.
Because I still remember the feeling I got when I looked, and there stood my Dad.

Chain Reaction

A gentler soul than Tommy Biddix, my Dad, one would hardly ever meet along life's way.
Courteous, helpful, and caring, not given to anger, rarely was his temper on display.

Such was not the case in 1959 when coming home from a road job snow began to fall, and the road started to freeze.
So, with several mountains to negotiate, he stopped to buy a set of chains at the only place he found open in Newport, Tennessee.

Now in those days, a good set of car chains, even at a gas station, sold for ten to twelve dollars at the most.
When Dad asked how much for a set of chains to fit his pickup, the man said twenty-five would be the cost.

Dad's anger welled up, told the man where to stick his chains that he would do just fine.
Said, before I pay your price, I'll wade snow up to my eyeballs on my way to Spruce Pine.

The old man shrugged as Dad stormed out the door, got in his truck, drove into the ditch and got stuck in the snow.
Calming down, he sized up the situation, realizing there was not much else to do. He would have to eat some crow.

So, back inside, he trudged, said I believe I'll take them chains since I'm having such bad luck.
The old-timer spat and said, I figured you would, but now the price has changed to thirty bucks.

I'm sure he felt like knocking the old-codger off his stool but seeing all the snow and ice,
He reached in his pocket, pulled out his billfold, and paid the old geezer his price.

I never heard Tommy Biddix say but two curse words, thinking back as far as I could.
I don't know if he said any that day. But if that situation didn't bring the cuss words, I doubt anything would.

My Dad was a heck of a man. I see in my two sons, grandson, and me a lot of his qualities I admire.
But when he told me this story, you could still see in him the righteous anger, passion, and fire.

Dad and My First Car

The week after I was sixteen, on a Saturday,
Daddy bought me my first car, a 1952 Bel Air Chevrolet.

As we went to Marion, NC my excitement I could not hide,
We drove into the Chevrolet dealership, and there sat my new ride.

Two tone blue and white, radio, heater, new seat covers, the works,
No dents, no scratches, low mileage, white walls, and fender skirts.

Daddy paid the salesman, did the paperwork, and out to the car we started to walk.
When suddenly he faced me, stopped, and said let's talk.

He said, son, I trust you, and this is a very special day.
But you need to do some things right, or that car goes away.

First and foremost, don't go driving crazy, and acting like a fool,
Also, you keep your grades up, do well in school.

Here are the keys, now I hope what I've told you really sinks in
Or quick as a hiccup, you'll be walking again.

I had tears in my eyes as I hugged and thanked my Dad.
Thinking back on the times, it probably took all the money he had.

I just bought a 2017 Ford Escape with all the bells, and whistles, drove it home the other day.
Solid red, black interior, turbo charged, great mileage, so they say.

But Dad, I know you are looking down from Heaven, and I want you to know,
That nothing will ever compare to the "52" Chevy you bought me long ago.

Medals in the Closet

I've often written of my Dad, Tommy, how in my life he played a huge part.
His untimely death at age sixty-four left a massive hole in my heart.

Dad was in World War II, a soft-spoken man of The Greatest Generation.
Leaving home and family to fight the Germans, he did his part to help save this nation.

None of his experiences did he talk about, nor did he want any accolades.
A true patriot, he would take offense at being called a hero, he never marched in any parades.

Being very interested In WW2, there was so much from him I wanted to learn.
But my Dad said very little, accepted no credit, said the heroes were those that did not return.

After Dad died, my mother lived with my sister, a lot of his things were packed away.
When my mother died, my sister, Polly, and I were going through some old boxes one day.

We found a child's shoe box within another box, faded and very old.
Inside: battle ribbons, bar, and medals, some silver, some gold.

Neither of us had seen them before, nor heard them talked about.
I remember thinking, it's a wonder over the years they had not been thrown out.

Now my sister was not a responsible person, but she said she would put them away.
I should have resisted because after she died, we haven't found them to this day.

It aggravated me for a while that she would be so careless with what was so precious to me.
But on reflection, I think somewhere, Dad smiled, for that's the way he wished it to be.

I imagine he never knew that my mother packed the medals and ribbons up one day.
I'll bet he didn't know where they were, probably thinking he threw them away.

Dad served God and Country quietly, faithfully, never seeking recognition or fame.
He left for me, his grandsons and great-grandson a living legacy. May we strive to do the same.

My Dad, LAX, and Johnny Cash

(My Last Trip With Dad)

My Dad, Tommy Biddix, in January of 1975, got the bad news that everyone dreads.
Cancer, spreading fast, very little can be done, less than a year to live, the doctor said.

In the spring of that year when things settled down, at least as much as they could be,
Dad and Mother left the Mountains for a while to visit us in Tennessee.

So, it was while they were staying Dad was surprised one day,
When I told him, "get up early tomorrow, we are going to LA."

Dad had never flown on a jet, and I doubt he slept much that night.
Next morning about seven, we were buckled in our first-class seats for the flight.

It was almost time to depart, the flight attendant informed us at last,
When suddenly a big man came in the door. It was Johnny Cash!

He nodded at Dad and me and sat down to our left in a window seat.
After take-off they served us breakfast, but Dad was too excited to eat.

I sat back and smiled, and a tear formed as I thought maybe at least for today,
Seeing Johnny Cash, and this airplane ride, hopefully, will keep the thought of cancer away.

On the three-hour trip, I tried to point out things about the airplane and some of the sights.
But Dad was interested in Johnny Cash, and hardly took his eyes off him the entire flight.

We landed in Los Angles, and since it was a one-day trip, there was not much we could do or see.
We looked around the airport, got some lunch, then boarded the non-stop back to Nashville about three.

It was a strenuous day, but Dad had a ball and for the first time in a long time,
He was talking continuously, and the twinkle was back in his eyes when we landed about nine.

Back in those days, in Nashville, to get to where we parked, everyone rode the same bus.
As it happened, our flight crew rode to the parking lot with us.

I knew the pilot, although his name I can't recall, and introduced him to my Dad.
They talked like old friends, and the Captain smiled when Dad told him about the day he had.

In a touch of irony, that kind Captain, and how I wish I could think of his name,
Died about two months before my Dad with a tumor on his brain.

Dad went to his grave, remembering and talking about that unforgettable day. His first flight in a jetliner, seeing Johnny Cash and flying into LA.

I miss you, Dad.

CHAPTER 4

Grandpa John Lowery - A True Man of the Mountains

John Alexander Lowery was born in 1869 and lived to be 96 years old. His father, Thomas Alexander Lowery, survived the Civil War, serving as a Sergeant in the Calvary under General Lee. Grandpa had nine children, my mother, the youngest. He was a strong, gentle man, a farmer that in his 96 years, never traveled more than fifty miles from where he was born. (e.g. "Way Over in Madison"). He and Grandma Lowery came to live with us in 1949. She died in 1952. He was and still is a significant influence in my life. Some people may take offense when I call Grandpa an "old man," but rest assured it is said with adoration, devotion, respect, and heartfelt undying love. A day does not pass that I don't think of him and miss him.

John Alexander Lowery

I was born in 1943, and it must have been the third or fourth year of my life,
I became aware of Grandpa, who was then past sixty-five.

To me, he seemed a giant of a man standing rugged and tall.
John Lowery was a true-hearted man of the Blue Ridge Mountains, born in 1869, early in the fall.

His father, Thomas Lowery, was a Calvary Sergeant with General Robert E. Lee,
But Great Grandpa Thomas never talked about the Civil War, at least that's what Grandpa told me

My dad was in World War Two and through most of my early years,
Grandpa was the one I went to for help with problems and fears.

When Grandma died, he came to live with us in 1949,
The fifteen years he lived with us passed so fast, it seemed like a short time.

We worked together, hoeing corn, raising a garden, cutting lots of wood,
He kidded me about my girlfriends, and he always wanted me to drive him when I could.

He lived ninety-six years in the mountains and never did roam,
More than fifty miles in any direction from the place he called home.

I cried when he died, and I still shed a tear today,
For John Lowery, my Grandpa, and each time I pray,

I am thankful that God allowed me a few years with this tough old mountain man,
He is a large part of who I am today, and I believe that was part of the Master's plan.

Now my steps are slow. I am nearly seventy-six years old.
My life will soon be a story that has been told,

When I die I know I will go to heaven, it's not that long until the trip,
As I approach the golden shore, Grandpa will welcome me, I know, with "I've been waiting for you, Skip."

Grandpa and the Constitution

In my home state of North Carolina, in 1959, to the best of my recollection,
A law was passed that you had to prove you could read to vote in the next election.

Now anyone could see this was a racist attack,
To suppress the vote of anyone that was black.

This meant everyone that wanted to vote had to register again at city hall.
So, I took my Grandpa Lowery to re-register, and he was very upset about it all.

Now Grandpa was 93, a strong old mountain man everyone respected.
Always voted in every election, and his vote was coveted by all that got elected.

When we got there, I filled out the paperwork because his hands shook.
Then they told Grandpa to read and handed me this massive, thick book.

It was the Constitution with the Preamble in big, bold print you could see three feet away.
But Grandpa wasn't quite ready to read yet, and he told them he had something to say.

I know why you are doing this, and it fills me with disgust and shame.
Any citizen of this country has the right to vote, no matter his color or name.

I held the Constitution for Grandpa, and in a firm voice he began to read,
"We the people" Grandpa read, and the registrar stepped in. You can stop, Mr. Lowery, he said, that's all we need.

Grandpa squared his shoulders and said, "no, that's not all you need.
You brought me in for this silly law, so by gosh, I'm gonna read!"

With great dignity, John Lowery read all the Preamble and started in on Article One!!
Sensing we might be there quite a while, I said, "you've made your point Grandpa, let's go home."

As we left the registrar said, "sorry Mr. Lowery, but the law says this is what you have to do,"
That don't make it right, son, Grandpa said, and you know that too.

We drove back home in silence and loving him as long as I had,
I could not remember ever seeing Grandpa so mad.

I'm a grown man now, many years have passed, and I often think of that day.
And it angers me to see voting suppression, although now it's manifest in other ways.

Closing of polling places, show your papers and stopping early voting are just a few I would note.
Grandpa knew, as do I, America is stronger and better for all if more people can vote.

Grandpa on the Go

In 1959 Mitchell County North Carolina had never seen so much snow and wind.
Grandpa Lowery was getting cabin fever because, at home, we were snowed in.

Now Grandpa only traveled from home in a radius of about fifty miles,
But he really enjoyed going to see his other eight children once in a while.

After we had been inside about six days, I saw how bad he wanted to go,
So, I got a shovel and spent the next four-or-five-hours shoveling snow.

I finally shoveled out the routes and got to the main gravel road that was clear.
Went back in the house, took a shower, and said to Grandpa, "let's get out of here."

He already had a few things packed in a little bag, much like a carry-on.
I put chains on my 1952 Chevy, and we were off to Aunt Cora's down in Marion.

I could tell he was pleased to be down out of those hills,
And before I started back, he winked and slipped me a dollar bill.

Did I take it? Of course, I did, and before you ask...
I was a teenager, and back then, that dollar bought four gallons of gas.

I drove back home, tired, worn out, muscles sore in every place.
But everything I did was worth it, to see the smile on Grandpa's face.

I know I've said it before, and I'll say it again and again,
Only God knows how much I loved that old man.

Grandpa the Weatherman

It was one of those beautiful days in the Blue Ridge Mountains, not a cloud in the sky.
The sky was so blue, the air so clear that you could see a bird if it was flying a mile high.

I was not taking in the beauty around me, though; my mind was on the hated task at hand.
Along with my Grandpa Lowery, I was doing what I hated most, hoeing corn on that steep hillside land.

It was about three in the afternoon, and this was the second of four days it would take us to get done.
As we took a water break, I saw Grandpa looking intently across the mountains and at the rows yet to come.

Best do all we can today, Skip, he said.
It'll be raining tomorrow, and we can stay in bed.

Well, because of my love for that old man, I kept my mouth shut, not telling him of my many doubts.
But looking now for the first time at the beautiful day, I thought old man; you don't know what you are talking about.

We worked until about seven, went home to Mama's good meal, and hit the sack about nine.
At least two more days of hoeing and thinking it might take even more time.

That night I slept the sleep of an extremely wearied person, no matter if an adult or a youth.
Then about three in the morning, I heard a clap of thunder and the drumbeat of rain falling on the tin roof.

Good old Grandpa, I thought as I pulled the covers up around my chin and smiled.
I could sleep late and enjoy the day. This mountain rain meant no more hoeing, at least for a while.

I end this poem about Grandpa as I have again and again:
Only God and I know how much I loved that old man.

Grandpa vs. the Government

Mitchell County, NC, is in the Blue Ridge Mountains, mountains being the operative word in play.
Flatland, land that is good for farming, one does not run across every day.

My Grandpa Lowery owned plenty of hillsides, but on top of one ridge was some of the flattest lands around.
So, into this picture in the 1930s came the National Park Service, wanting to buy this piece of ground.

The Blue Ridge Parkway was coming through that stretch, the government man said.
Then proceeded to make Grandpa a lowball offer that left him scratching his head.

You see, Grandpa sometimes worked up in Little Switzerland for Judge
Clarkson, cutting grass and such.
The Judge had some land the Parkway was going to take also, but according to
Grandpa, not as much.

As I understand it, the Judge had been offered more for a whole lot less.
Grandpa, with this knowledge in his pocket, told the government men he
didn't think their offer met the test.

I can imagine the look on these men's faces as they sat there in that cabin
across from Grandpa in his overalls.
Thinking they were going to put one over on this old mountain man, now
they were the ones taking the fall.

I don't know how much he got. I know he used the money to buy more land,
including the place where Uncle Slim built our home when Dad came back
from the war.
And now, occasionally, when we go back home, we drive that flat stretch of
road and remember when Grandpa sent the government men packing, never
to be seen anymore.

As I end, I'll say what I always say again and again,
God only knows how I loved that old man.

Grandpa, Tobacco, and Me

I've written about my Grandpa Lowery and my love for that old man.
He chewed Sampson's Tobacco; it came in a twist, not in a can.

I don't remember how old I was, probably twelve, thirteen or so,
We were hoeing corn together, a job I really hated, as you know.

I was beating the dirt and sweating as we worked that hard ground.
I stopped, thought for a moment, then slowly turned around.

I said, "if I'm old enough to work and sweat out here with you,
Seems to me that I would be old enough to chew."

Grandpa spit, wiped his brow, and said, "Skip, I guess you are right."
Reached in his overalls, took out the twist, and told me to take a bite.

Timidly I bit just a little off the end, thinking that would be enough.
But Grandpa said, "no," and I filled up my jaw with that stuff.

Slowly, slowly, ever so slowly, I began to chew.
I started sweating, gagging, getting dizzy, and I didn't know what to do.

Next thing I knew, I was down in the cornrows of dirt and dust.
And there on my knees, I started puking up my guts.
When I got to feeling some better, I told Grandpa I had better go home.
He said, "no, Skip, finish up the field, we're far from being done."

I saw him kind of grinning as I started back to hoeing the corn.
And I still don't know how I made the rest of the day on the farm.

Life's lessons are learned in many ways.
And I learned one that has served me very well since that day.

Understand your limits, what you can and cannot do.
Or sometimes you will find that you will bite off more than you can chew.

Grandpa, Watching Girls Go By

When I was growing up long ago and, in another time,
The closest small town to us was called Spruce Pine.

Every week when Saturday rolled around,
I took Mama, Polly, and Grandpa into town.

Grandpa and I were in my car waiting on the other two and talking,
When down the street came two young ladies, about twenty, "walking."

They were very well built with all body parts truly proportioned,
And as they walked, their backfields were definitely in motion.

Now for the ladies, Grandpa Lowery always had a keen eye.
And he never took his eyes off these two as they went by.

He turned to me and said just as they turned the corner and went out of sight,
Skip, if I was twenty years younger, we could sure have us some fun tonight.

Grandpa was then in his mid-nineties, so, in my mind, I did the subtraction.
Hmm, I thought, that would make him about seventy-four if we swung into action.

Now I'm seventy-six and when I reflect on that day,
Will I reach ninety-six as he did? Nope, there is no way!

But hope springs eternal, I will remember Grandpa and think that I can.
Another one of a thousand reasons why I loved that old man.

Ice Cream and Grandpa

Local politicians regularly came to our house when I was young.
They wanted my Grandpa's blessing, for the race they were going to run.

A long-winded politico finally got up to leave one day,
And flipped me a nickel as he went on his way.

Get you an ice cream bar at school tomorrow, he said with a grin.
Grandpa spat and said that boy likes dime ice cream now and then.

The politician frowned and went into his pocket once more,
And flipped me a quarter as he walked out the door.

Wow!! Thirty cents I now had as I looked in my hand.
Grandpa Lowery just winked. God only knows how I loved that old man.

Way Over in Madison

Grandpa Lowery did not talk a whole lot, so I always listened when he spoke.
It was usually a story he told about his life growing up. I don't think I ever heard him tell a joke.

He spoke with authority, but often with a twinkle or sadness in his eye,
As he told about the good times and the bad times of days gone by.

As a small boy, I spent a lot of time with Grandpa and listened carefully when he began to talk.
One thing that always fascinated me was that almost everywhere he went, he would walk.

Now I don't think, but once in his life, he traveled more than fifty miles from his little mountain farm.
And that was to Winston Salem Hospital for an operation he recovered from.

When he was in his late eighties, and Mama needed cornmeal, flour, sugar or something more,
And Daddy was at work with our only car; Grandpa would say I'll just "step" up to the store.

Now Little Switzerland Store was a good two miles away.
Oh, and it was a steady climb on a crooked, narrow roadway

So that was four miles of walking, plus carrying whatever in his sack.
I went with him one time at age nine and was worn out when we got back.

He often talked about the time he worked as a hired hand,
For a man in another county, to Grandpa a far distant land.

Madison County was only about thirty miles and three counties away to the west of Spruce Pine.
But to hear Grandpa tell it, that was about as far as you could go in this vast world at that time.

He would spit and tell about the time he "went WAY over in Madison" to work for this man.
And to a small boy, like me, that hung on every word, I just knew that had to be as far as you could go in this land.

When we return to the Mountains now, I smile, a lump comes in my throat, and I go back in time.
Because between Asheville and Spruce Pine, just like always, we cross the Madison County Line.

I brush a tear aside as I think of that Grand Old Man I loved so much as he talked about "Madison" land.
And now he has gone to Heaven to live far beyond the stars in a mansion so beautiful and grand!!

See you soon, Grandpa!

Grandpa's Birthday

Memory is both a wonderful and painful thing as age begins to take its toll. Some memories make you smile; some seem to bring on the tears as we grow old.

One of the happiest times of my youth that I can recall,
Is when we celebrated my Grandpa Lowery's birthday late in the fall.

On the first Sunday in October, the family would gather to honor Grandpa on his special day.
A time when all of his grandchildren, my cousins, and I would get together and play.

I remember the celebration being held at Uncle Bascomb's, Aunt Cora's, and a few times at our home.
Why sometimes as many as one hundred people would come and see Grandpa before the day was gone.

I remember the older men would smoke, spit, whittle, and talk about the war. The younger men and some of us kids would listen to the World Series from a radio in a car.

The sisters and other ladies talked about everything and everybody as they prepared the feast.
And everyone waited anxiously with great anticipation to hear the magic words, "let's eat!"

But first, the blessing, usually given by a preacher or the oldest relative of Grandpa still around.
And us children also prayed, that whoever said the blessing would soon shut up and sit down.

We wanted some of that food, and it was a meal fit for presidents and kings. Everything that bountiful mountain gardens had produced and anything else they could bring.

There was plenty of fried chicken, ham, Mama's chicken and dumplings, Aunt Nell's homemade pies.
Corn, green beans, potatoes, okra, cakes of all kinds, and casseroles of every size.

But Grandpa always looked for something my cousin Bobby Lowery had brought just for him:
A mess of squirrels Bobby had killed and had Mama cook, even though squirrel season was never in.

I can still see Grandpa smiling as the day went on, and folks kept coming by. A man of few words, you could tell how happy he was by the twinkle in his eyes.

Grandpa is gone now, along with his nine children, their spouses, and most of my cousins. Only a few of us remain.
Oh, we still gather in August, thanks to Bootsie's daughter Brenda, but somehow, it's not the same.

Each year on the first Sunday in October, no matter where I happen to be, I pause, look toward the mountains, think of Grandpa, and those Mountain people that mean so much to me.

And I thank God for where I came from, those that helped me become the man that I am today.
Someday very soon, I'll see them and personally thank them for their help

along the way.

But whenever that day comes, and these days the way I feel it's not going to be a long wait,
I know Grandpa, with a twinkle in his eye, will welcome me with "I've been waiting on you, Skip."

Grandpa's Wooden Coffin

If you have read much of what I have written over the years,
Then you know that my Grandpa Lowery was someone very dear.

As he advanced into his nineties, he did not speak of his imminent death often.
But I once heard him say it was his wish to be buried in a homemade wooden coffin.

So, at some point earlier, I don't know how old he was or exactly when,
He made arrangements to be fitted and have a coffin made by my Uncle Slim.

A carpenter in high demand in Little Switzerland, NC, was my Uncle Slim,
He lived close by, loved Grandpa, and was always visiting him.

I guess not many in our huge family knew that the coffin was done,
And stored waiting for Grandpa in a Marion, NC, funeral home.

Johnny, my first cousin, Uncle Slim's son, told me what his dad had done,
But, surprisingly, we were to keep it to ourselves and not tell anyone.

The secrecy seemed strange to me, and I wondered why we had to keep quiet.
Then at age ninety-six Grandpa passed away, and the wooden coffin almost caused a riot.

Seems some in our large family wanted a fancy coffin, saying it looked more dignified.
Ignoring Grandpa's wishes on what he wanted buried in when he died.

But the furor died down, common sense prevailed, and the service went on as planned.
And I remember sitting in church thinking how that rough but beautiful wood mirrored his life span.

Grandpa's been gone many years now. Soon I'll see him once again, hug him, and shake his hand.
But for now, I'll close with what I have said before: *Only God knows how I loved that Old Man.*

Goodbye Grandpa

It was August 1964; I don't recall the exact day,
When I got the news in Washington, DC, that Grandpa Lowery passed away.

Margaret and I left the Mountains a year before, starting our lives together as man and wife.
We loaded all we had in a 1952 Chevy, traveling to our Nation's Capital to work for the FBI.

The phone call came early in the morning, around the break of day.
We hurriedly packed for NC, not knowing how long we would stay.

My '52 Chevy was worn out, and I was afraid it would not make the one-thousand-mile trip this time.
My good friend, Larry Boyd, had a new 1963 Ford and, without hesitation, pitched me the keys and said, "take mine."

I don't remember the drive or when we got back to what had been my home.
I do remember thinking the road had never seemed that long.

We got there just as the hearse was bringing Grandpa's body to his room where he would lie for a couple of days.
They often did that with funerals back then; it was a part of Mountain customs and ways.

There was a crowd of relatives gathered that greeted us with tears and open arms.
While I appreciated that, I soon slipped away and walked by myself up to the barn.

I found an old wooden box to sit on, opened the latch on a stall, and went inside.
Unashamed, I sat there, looking up to Heaven, deep in thought, broken-hearted, and cried.

I thought of this Old Man I loved, lying in the homemade wooden coffin in the room where he always slept.
Of the nights, I was in the other bed and would be at his side if he needed any help.

I thought of the nights when I couldn't sleep and listening to see if he was all right.
I would say, "Grandpa," he would say, "What Skip" quickly, no matter the time of night.

I sat there thinking of words, such as I love you, words I wish I had said that were now too late to say.
I know he knew I loved him, but unfortunately, I guess it's a man thing, and it's just not our way.

We buried John Alexander Lowery, my Grandpa, not far from where he spent his life.
At Turkey Cove Baptist Church Cemetery alongside Lula, his loving wife.

He never traveled a long way from his home in the Mountains, raised a family of nine children, was honest and true.
A part of Americana was buried that day, one of the old-timers, the backbone of our country, now that number very few.

I thank God I was with him here on earth, and before long I know I can,
See him in Heaven, but until then, as I've said many times, only God knows how I loved that Old Man.

Coming to see you soon, Grandpa!!

CHAPTER 5

Faith is Fundamental

My Faith was formed early in my life in the mountains. In these writings, you will find people and events that have shaped me into the man I am today, stories of fears, doubts, wrong actions, and redemption. I hope in these poems, you can identify with some of the people that have inspired and helped me in good times and bad. It is also my prayer that words written on these pages lead you to the One that is the Source of all comfort and hope.

A Follower That Fails

Lord, It's your servant Ed coming before You yet again,
Asking Your forgiveness, confessing all my sins.

I answered the call to follow You way back in my teenage years.
You saved me, protected me, and calmed all my fears.

Your love is unconditional; You never condemn, shame, or turn me away.
It's me that disappoints You, God, as I confess to You today.

You know my weaknesses, Heavenly Father, my thoughts, and what I have done.
Sins I have struggled with, battles, and problems I have yet to overcome.

So help me Lord, to love You more, once again may I feel the joy,
And recapture that simple faith I had when You saved me as a boy.

Help me to put You first in my life, not the things of this world I hold dear.
May I focus on what's eternal and not the possessions I will leave down here.

And thank You, I can start over each day, forgiven, clean, and new.
And dear God, may I strive to be a better follower and not a disappointment to You.

A Conversation With God

I got a call from an old friend, and we met for lunch the other day.
He said he was going through a time where it was hard for him to pray.

He was having some problems, but knowing him I thought it kind of odd,
That he would be having trouble in his prayer life and talking to God.

I sat in silence as he related his problems; all he had been through.
And wondered what I would say when he asked me what he should do.

He said he had prayed and prayed, but somehow got the feeling,
That his earnest pleas reached no higher than the ceiling.

Finally, I said, I hear you. I know you are praying and pouring your heart out to God each day.
But have you paused, and taken time to listen to what God and the Holy Spirit have to say?

He looked puzzled, so I asked what we had been doing ever since we sat down.
Talking and having a conversation, he said with a frown.

You're right, I said to my friend.
And a conversation means you have to listen now and then.

Pray and then pause reverently, listen to what God has to say.
You need to hear Him. He already knew your request anyway.

It's also good to find a quiet place, humble yourself, and don't be too proud,
To talk to Him just like you are talking to me, eyes open and out loud.

I haven't seen him since, so I don't know if he took my advice or not.
But sometimes a simple give and take with our Savior sure helps a lot.

Revival in the Mountains

In the Blue Ridge Mountains back in the fifties, sixties, and a long, long time before then,
Revivals were held, and a traveling evangelist came to preach and remind us of our sin.

The services were held in tents and sometimes in our church down by the creek.
Usually, they lasted about ten days, but if the "spirit" was moving, maybe three or four weeks.

It seems in those days that the revival preachers all fit the profile of being solemn, tall, and thin.
That is until he started preaching. Then a transformation happened, and a

totally different person stepped in.
He would stride back and forth, pounding the pulpit, his face distorted and red,
Spit flying from his mouth, eyes darting everywhere, ready to pop out of his head!

He said we were all sinners, and only Christ could forgive and set us free.
When I raised my head to look up, he was pointing a bony finger right at me.

As I sat there for what felt like hours, I had never felt so alone.
He had convinced me I was going to hell, probably before I got home.

I made it home though and sweated through a sleepless night.
So, imagine my surprise the next day when I saw his car come in sight.

Mama had invited him to come to our house for lunch at noon.
To my surprise, a much different man than the night before came into the living room.

He was soft-spoken, a perfect gentleman, didn't yell, or scream at all.
Why even after lunch, we went outside and tossed a baseball.

But I kept watching the reverend out of the corner of my eye,
Wondering if he would give me a clue about when I was going to die.

He stayed until about three and not once did he mention or tell,
Mama or relatives and neighbors who came by that I was surely bound for hell.

He left in about a week, and I've never seen him again to this day.
I didn't end up in hell, slept better at night, and my fears went away.

He did plant a seed, though at that young age, I didn't know what that meant at all.
And about two years later, in a different service, I answered the Holy Spirits call.

I am an old man now, and I like to think about and look back on my childhood days.
And reflect on how God uses many people and different methods to

accomplish His ways.
We need to be aware of those people God uses to tell others about Him as we walk in this world below.
They may not look like we think they should, act like we think they should, or go where we think they should go.

But if they present the true Gospel, have compassion, and love ALL people as well,
Then we should pray for and support them because it just might keep some young person from going to hell.

There is also a lesson here that we must consider and apply to our lives before we are through.
If God can use anyone to tell others about Him, then that would mean he could use me, and he could use you.

Thank God for Unanswered Prayer

In February of 1996, at the ripe old age of fifty-three,
I found out I was going to be a Grandpa. I was as happy as one can be.

Problems developed in our daughter-in-law's pregnancy, and we began to fear.
Then the doctor said the baby would have to be taken, even though two months premature.

Teresa was hospitalized, very sick with preeclampsia, pain, and worry.
The doctors hesitated to do a C-section, but she said, please, hurry.

On February 22, sometime around one,
Aaron came into this world, my only Grandson.

He was so beautiful, yet at just three pounds, so tiny and small,
He was so fragile and driving home; I wondered if he would live at all.

That night as I prayed to God, I started out thanking Him for all the blessings I had.
But before I realized it, I found myself getting mad.

I couldn't bear the thought that my Grandson might die,
So, in earnest prayer and anger to God, I began to cry.

Lord, I said, you know me, my life, my sin.
I ain't no bargain to you, never have been.

But that little guy lying there in the hospital bed,
He's never done anything wrong or had a bad thought in his head.

So tonight, if someone in Heaven with You has to be,
Then please, Lord, let Aaron live and take me.

Well, it's 2019, I just turned seventy-six, and Aaron is twenty-three,
And what a joy these many years having my Grandson with me.

And I'm often reminded when I pray,
Of the prayers answered and unanswered that day.

So, I can truthfully say when we are put to the test,
Let God decide, for he always knows best.

An Angel at Sam's Club

I was standing in line to checkout at Sam's Club. Christmas was a few weeks away.
Told a few hours earlier that I had prostate cancer, I was having an awful day.

As I took my place in the checkout lane, with head bowed, I thought my turn at the register would take a very long time.
However, due to the efficient and smiling young black checkout lady, very soon, I was next in line.

Sir, she said I'm sorry that you had to stand and wait so long.
And pardon me for asking, but you look as if something is wrong.

I nodded, told her I had been to the doctor, and he gave me some bad news,
I would need an operation after the first of the year, due to urgent health issues.

She looked at my Sam's card, Edwin Tommy Biddix, it read.
She asked what name I went by; I said, just call me Ed.

She smiled, took my hand, and said Ed, here's what I'm going to do.
From now on, you are in my prayers, I am going to pray for you.

I paid for my items and mumbled thanks, thank you for your prayer,
And brushing back a tear, I stepped out into the wintry December air.

I remember getting in my car and humbly thanking God for what that beautiful young lady said.
Now the day seemed brighter, my spirits were lifted, and I suddenly saw better days ahead.

The operation went fine. I had an excellent surgeon and incredible hospital care.
I went back to Sam's to thank the young lady, but she was not there.

Each time I go to Sam's, I look for her; however, my search always ends in vain.
Many times, I have been back to that store, yet I have never seen her again.

I think God has unique people he sends to us as we travel life's highway.
Angels unaware I call them, and one encouraged me that day.

God's in the Skyscraper

I was having some problems in my life, and the future looked grim.
So, I sought out an elderly friend to get some advice from him.

I told him my problems, and as he answered I became afraid,
He didn't understand my problem or hear a word that I said.

He looked at me intently and asked this question that made me frown:
Have you ever taken your boys to the Christmas parade downtown?

Downtown was Nashville, Tennessee, Music City USA,
About twenty-five miles from Murfreesboro, where we still live today.

Boy, I thought, did he misunderstand what I had to say?
What a stupid question to ask, and I started to walk away.

But respect for him and his opinion told me to wait and understand what he meant.
Thank God I did because he gave me remarkable advice I have lived by ever since.

I told him yes, several years had gone by since we did the Christmas parade bit.
Then came another seemingly foolish question, where did you sit?

Now thoroughly convinced he did not know what he was talking about,
I told him in front of Union Station, right in the middle of the parade route.

And what did you observe, he asked with a grin,
Could you see the beginning, could you see the end?

No, I answered, just what was passing in front of my eyes.
Correct, he said, that's how you and I live our lives.

But you must realize son; God watches that parade from the Life and Casualty Tower's (LCT) top floor,
He views the beginning and the end, you and I look at what passes in front of us, and no more.

Now, at that time, the LCT, a skyscraper, was the tallest building in town.
And from its tower, you could identify everything for miles around.

So, hang in there, he said, believe God's promises forever, from first to last.
And also remember there is a lot of truth in the old saying, this too shall pass.

I try my best to live by what that wise fella advocates,
And think of him fondly each time I watch parades.

I Haven't... However...

Dear God, not one bad thought has crossed my mind today.
I haven't said anything that would lead anyone astray.

A curse word has yet to pass my lips.
No slanderous talk, no smart mouth quips.

I haven't coveted, lied, or cheated my fellowman.
Actually, I've been just about as perfect as anyone can.

So, I'm not worried as long as I'm feeling and acting this way.
However, I'm putting my feet on the floor, getting up for the first time today.

Then, God, the struggle with all things evil will begin,
And I'll need You every second until I go to sleep again.

Prayer

Why do we take some things for granted? It's something we do all the time. Take prayer, for example. As much as I try to keep in touch with the Almighty, many days I find,

That it seems I am too busy to stop and take time to pray.
Rush, rush, rush, and other priorities take precedent that day.

But wait. We, humans, are such a piece of work as we walk life's highway.
What if God didn't have time for us, turned His back, and went away?

Still, I think we pray more than we think we do though we may not pray very long.
Thanks, is always a one-word prayer when said to God above. Prayer can also be humming a religious song.

Help me, Lord, you may quickly say as you navigate the traffic on the interstate.
And a simple thank you, Jesus, as you make it to your appointment only two minutes late.

But there are times when we get serious with God as we wait for the tests to come back.
He comforts us as we promise Him we will not ever again let our prayer life get off track.

And when those tests come back, negative or positive, He is always there.
He never left you. He understands. You are and will always be in His care.

So, let's try to do better in our prayer life. Get back into regular prayer and Bible study once more.
Life happens, and it's much better to be "prayed up" the next time trouble comes knocking on the door.

Oh, and when it comes to prayer, we need to remember it is a conversation with God above all else.
And having a conversation means listening to Him and not doing all the talking yourself.

A Sore Throat From Heaven

Those that know me know my dad, Tommy Biddix, was a hero of mine.
Passing away at age 64 with cancer, he left us way before his time.

We all knew, Christmas of 1976, would be his last on this earth with us.
And I had been trying my best to get off work, but my efforts had been a total bust.

You see, I worked for American Airlines in Nashville, Tennessee.
And my dad lived 300 miles away in the mountains of Western NC.

In the airline business, Christmas time is the busiest part of the year.
Vacations are limited, all hands on deck, time off is rare.

But three days before Christmas, I got out of bed with a very sore throat.
Otherwise, I was feeling just fine. No fever, cough, nor anything else to note.

Still, for Christmas, I wanted to be well.
So, before my afternoon shift, I went to see Dr. Fridell.

Ed, he said, you've got strep throat. You certainly don't need to be out in this cold air.
He prescribed antibiotics, gave me a shot, and suddenly a thought hit me as I stood there.
Doc, I said, am I contagious, and he said no, you are not.

Could I possibly travel if I was careful and was not out a lot?

I told him the situation, how much I wanted to spend Christmas with my dad.
Dr. Friddell nodded, wrote a note for work, and gave it to me along with the prescriptions from his pad.

I went home, we got the boys and presents together and loaded up the car.
About six hours and three hundred miles later, we were in the mountains sitting by dad's fire.

Christmas that year was bittersweet, but at least we got to be with him on his last Christmas Day.
Nearly four months later, as spring came to the mountains, Tommy Biddix, my father, passed away.

Now some would say that my sore throat just happened, that I got the virus off some doorknob.
That may be true, but I will always believe with all my heart, it was the act of a loving, caring God.

Hats in Church

When it comes to going to church, I'm "old school" in a lot of ways.
I like to sing and hear the old songs of worship and praise.

I realize that Rock of Ages and Amazing Grace are not everyone's cup of tea.
So, a mixture of the old and new songs the young folks like is just fine with me.

The order of the service doesn't bother me one bit.
I have no favorite pew, could care less where I sit.

There is one thing I get upset about, a visual I can barely abide.
That's when I see men wearing their caps inside.

Men remove their hats for the National Anthem at sporting events and such,

Why would they not have enough respect for God to take it off in church?

If I didn't ask the Lord to restrain me, I'm very much afraid,
Before he got settled in his seat, I'd snatch it off his head.

Respect, dignity, and reverence seem to be missing in houses of worship today.
Dress your best, remove that hat, and put aside anything that would hinder you or others as you pray.

Let's return to the old school way of worship, be aware of how we act and what we do.
Remember, Angels, walk among us, and every service Jesus sits beside you and me on the pew.

The Inward Voice

I do not doubt that sometimes God speaks to us. I think He does it in a variety of ways.
And I'm a wee bit leery of those that are quick to say God speaks audibly to them every few days.

And if you really want a piece of my mind this is what you do:
Come up to me and say: God told me to tell you.

No, l don't think that happened. Why would He do that I would have to say.
I talked to Him this morning, and He said nothing about you coming my way.

God communicates through His Word, nature, the Holy Spirit in a variety of ways.
I must admit, however, I heard a Voice that I cannot explain speak to me one day.

It was a week before the first of five operations I would undergo in the next five years.
It was a full knee replacement, and I approached the dreaded day with many doubts and fears.

I had just finished my Bible and prayer time in the sunroom, worried, starting

the day anew.
When suddenly I heard in my mind, "Do you or do you not believe what My Word tells you?"

Well, it was a powerful question, and stopping in my tracks, I whispered silently, "Yes, God, I do."
From that moment on, all fear was gone; the operation gave me a knee that was almost good as new.

As a matter of fact, as the nurse was getting me ready for surgery, she said she had never seen anyone so at ease.
I smiled and said, I am not worried, ma'am. The Greatest of all Physicians is going in the operating room with me.

So, here's the way I see it. God speaks to us in many ways, ways in which we often have no choice.
It could be a baby's cry, words of a wise man, a thunderstorm, or just maybe, A Still, Small, Voice.

The Face of God

When going to church in the mountains, often, men in the congregation were called on to pray.
Some prayed about politics and country, some the lost and sick. Some prayers were short, others, it seemed took all day.

There was one old gentleman; Uncle Buelow Hollifield was his name, an old-timer of about eighty-four,
Dressed in clean overalls, I really paid attention when he was called on for prayer.

Brushing back his snow-white hair, slowly he would rise,
Lifting his hands toward Heaven as he prayed, he never closed his eyes.

Lord, he would say, it's me talking to you again. With tears in his eyes, it seemed to me his face took on a glow.

Man, I thought he sees God; they are conversing face to face, like friends, like someone you honestly know.

He didn't pray long or use fancy words, as he spoke to the Father above.
He prayed for the lost, the healing of the sick, and thanked God for His love.

I remember seeing that old man, as clear as if it was yesterday, how his prayers reached beyond the sky.
Yet you and I can have that same pipeline to God today if we truly seek His face and try.

The Least of These

"In as much as you have done it unto THE LEAST OF THESE, you have done it unto Me."
So, who was He talking about as He taught the disciples how they should live and be?

I think we all know if we read the Bible, put our mind in gear and study His Word,
It was the poor, downtrodden, and outcasts among us whom He wants to be heard.

Probably the easiest way to discern who Jesus was talking about,
Is to read the Gospels and see where He was found hanging out.

Of course, we know He walked everywhere He went, there were no airplanes.
But had there been He would have condemned those buying them and using His name.

You didn't find Him in the palaces, and banks, with religious leaders or any political party at all.
His anger burned, and He overthrew the money changers and others out of the temple as I recall.

He believed those that worked deserved an honest day's pay.
And would condemn those that misuse and cheat employees today.

If He were here, He would be talking to that drunk in the bar down the street.
And telling how God loves and wants to help the junkies, He meets.

The runaway, the prodigal, the prostitute, He does not condemn or judge.
No one has sinned or fallen so far; they are out of the range of His love.

When you think of "the least of these" I'm sure it would be in order,
For Him to visit and cry over children in cages down at the border.

He would visit Shady Rest, Sunset Village, and other "rest homes,"
And comfort the older generation that is forgotten and alone.

And what about the old soldiers, in poor care because of broken promises at the VA.
He would love them, thank them, tell them to trust in Him for a home in Heaven one day.

Little children, He loves and likens them to His Heavenly Home.
So, likewise, He would be there beside those that are abused, beaten, and alone.

These are just a few of "the least of these" and only a small look at what Jesus would do.
We know who they are, the least of these. Now the question is: what are you…and I going to do?

Christians Without a Conscience??

America is a Christian Nation, so the statistics and the surveys say.
I'm afraid that may be in name only since many seem to act in an opposite way.

Now I'm not here to judge or cast dispersions, not anything like that.
I will leave that up to the Master and try to state the facts.

I guess as I grow older, I tend to see things in a different light.
The hypocrisy, the indifference, the inability to distinguish between wrong and right.

For instance, those that sing Oh How I Love Jesus in church as they pray,
And then refuse to help those in need that they see every day.

Or those that talk about their love and brotherhood for people of every race.
Then out of their site, call them names they would never say to their face.

All life is precious (and it is) they shout. Marches and protests are held in cities all day long.
The baby is born, yet effective programs cut, basically saying, "Hey kid, you are on your own."

So dear Mr. and Mrs. Christian, take stock of your conscience as you worship and pray each day.
Do your actions and your conscience back up your prayers, or are they just words that you say?

Corporations, people in business, as you worship God on the Sabbath day,
Did you make your vast profits on the backs of those workers at minimum pay?

Hey corporate farms that produce much of the vegetables that we eat in the USA,
Do you use illegals to work your crops, then yell for ICE to haul them away??

Fellow worshippers, citizens, Christians, Americans, people of all ages,
Did your conscious keep you from sleeping at night when they locked little children in cages?

Thousands dying each day in poverty, and we Christians dare to say, "the Lord called them home."
No, my friend. In large part, they died because of no healthcare, and poverty wages robbed them of the will to go on.

Now, these are just a few of the injustices that we see around us every day.
So, fellow Christian, does any of this affect your conscience as you pray?

If not, I think maybe I would get on my knees and ask why.
If Jesus walked with us, and He does, would He pass on by??

God, I thank you for all my blessings, and I pray that I may not be like the Pharisee and Scribe,
Upon seeing the man beaten, bleeding and dying there on the road turned

and passed by on the other side.

May I be like the Good Samaritan, Lord, and give me a conscience that cares. For who knows? Except for Your Grace, it might be me lying there.

CHAPTER 6

My Misspent (But Fun) Youth

Ah, the pleasures of youth! The joys of being a teenager, full of life, and bulletproof (or so we thought). In this chapter, I feel confident you will find writings relating to that pivotal time in your life when, as we look back, it was chaotic, but most of the time, a ball. Here you will find some of my high school friends, experiences, highlights, and embarrassing moments, I think, you can relate to and make you smile.

An Encounter That Lasted a Lifetime

As a junior in high school, Mr. Baker's Civics class ended about noon,
Upon dismissal, we ran down the hall like wild turkeys, with most of us football players going to the lunchroom.

I must have been in a hurry on this particular day,
Because I knocked down this young lady that got in my way.

I went back to help her and pick up her books.
She didn't say anything, just gave me a dirty look.

I told her how sorry I was again and again,
As she got to her feet, I looked at her and then. . .

Wow, I breathlessly thought as I kept apologizing, where has this girl been?
Long black hair, hourglass figure, she was the most beautiful girl I had ever seen.

Margaret Willis, she told me when I asked for her name.
I asked her out, we dated, and my life has never been the same.

Now it's nearly sixty years later since that fateful day,
And each time I see her, she still takes my breath away.

Don't run in the hall, our teachers would always say,
But I thank God I disobeyed them on that day.

Game Day, October 1960

Fall in the Blue Ridge Mountains, especially in Little Switzerland, NC,
The area is ablaze in color, beautiful foliage as far as you can see.

But beauty is not on my mind as I eat, dress for school, and start on my way.
You see, this is different from the other four days, Friday is Game Day.

That feeling in the pit of my stomach was there when I went to bed.
I had slept well, though, knowing I was prepared for the game that lay ahead.

Seeing my teammates and girlfriend when I got to school made the day move fairly fast.
The pep rally got everyone fired up, and we knew our opponents didn't stand a chance.

I'm afraid the day was wasted on me concerning what I had learned.
It was that big middle linebacker I would face at center that had me concerned.

The school day was over, and I drove home to Mama's early bird home-cooked meal.
You know how Mamas are, "you gotta eat Son, I don't care how amped up you feel."

Our opponent this night is Bakersville, the biggest game Mitchell County has seen.
They are our in-county rivals, and we hate each other. That's the way it's always been.

Tonight, will be only the second time we've played in seven years because of that fateful night,
When they said, police and fire trucks had to restore order and break up the riot.

Skyline A Conference banned the Blue Devils and Bulldogs playing for five years, a move that was smart.
Now in the second year back to playing, each team was itching to tear the other one apart.

Both teams are undefeated at midseason, but we have been barely winning on the road and at home.
While the Bulldogs have been trouncing everyone and had not even been scored upon.

That feeling in the pit of my stomach as we lined up for the kickoff was now an adrenaline high.
And as I raced down the field to hit someone, training replaced emotion as I threw a block and ran on by.

I won't bore you with the details of the game that we won twenty-four to seven.
Or how the Sheriff had to get us out of the mob, sometime around eleven.

No, I'll talk of the joy of winning and how everyone in Spruce Pine welcomed us that night.
Food was free at the City Cafe, and people were cheering, honking horns, it was an incredible sight!

I had a different feeling deep inside as we celebrated the win and a hard-fought fight.
Pride in my team, our little mountain town, myself, and a feeling that all in the world was right.

But Monday came, another week of school and practice began.
And come Thursday night, I knew I would get that feeling in my gut again.

It's many, many, years later; the leaves are beautiful, fall and football are on the way.
I am an old man now, but I would give up some of the time I have left for just one more Game Day.

Coach John Norton

In the fall of 1957, I went out for the football team, 14 years old and 145 pounds soaking wet.
We lined up in the gym in our shorts, and suddenly, in came the meanest looking man I ever met.

John Norton was his name, and he told us in no uncertain terms that he was boss.
He gave a speech about team, hard work, and discipline, and were we ready to pay the cost?

The trainer gave out uniforms to the upperclassmen that played before.
When all of those were dispersed, only four very raggedy sets were left, four and no more.

Coach Norton looked the rest of us over and started moving down the line. He handed the four uniforms out, as he looked at us, and there was one left after I got mine.

Then came another speech, this time on his face, he had a sadistic grin.
Don't be discouraged if you didn't get one, he said. There will be quitters that turn theirs in.

I remember exactly what I thought when he said that, precisely what went through my mind.
You won't get this one back, Coach, and I am going to make this team. This uniform is MINE!

One thing I need to tell you, playing football for the Harris High Blue Devils, was every boy's dream.
It was the biggest thing going in Spruce Pine. Everyone came to watch the team.

But back to Coach Norton, and little did I realize that on that day,
I was beginning a four-year journey with him that would impact me in so many ways.

His practices were rigid. He demanded perfection, and he was impossible to please.
But because of the way we had to practice, Friday night games were a breeze.

I played end and guard, sometimes at linebacker on defense.
But I found my true calling my last two years playing center on the offense.

The Coach was a solid taskmaster, and he had a brilliant football mind.
He could game plan to perfection and develop schemes unheard of at that time.

In addition to coaching, Mr. Norton taught history, a subject he liked and knew.
He walked the line between coaching and history and never mixed the two.

I learned so many life lessons from playing football and this man.
Lessons of perseverance, toughness, and how to be a better man.

After a demanding, exhausting, practice when our spirits and bodies screamed, we've had enough,
Coach walked up and down, saying, "Guys, this ain't nothing. Its life that's tough."

"When you think you've reached your limit when you feel you are about to tank,
Remember this day, reach deep down inside you. You still have something left in the bank."

He motivated in a lot of ways, sometimes I guess out of fear.
He was not much for compliments, few "good job" or praise did you hear.

Still, he's one of those people in my life that made me the man I am today.
And often, when life gets rough, the road gets hard, I remember what he had to say.

About three weeks before graduation, Coach Norton said, get your yearbook and come to my room at the end of the hall.
Outside of being in trouble, or messing up in football, I had never been in his office at all.

He put me at ease, though, as he motioned for me to sit down.
He looked up, and on his face was a smile instead of the usual frown.

Edwin, he said, for four years, you have done everything I asked you to do.
I appreciate the dedicated work, and I want you to know, you are ready for whatever life throws at you.

He asked for my yearbook and in, what was his abrupt style, scribbled a short note.
But the words of praise from this harsh old Coach meant more to me than anything he wrote.

I am now seventy-six years old, I've had good times, bad times, up, down, and all around.
Still, I pull from the things I learned years ago from Coach—some of the best advice to be found.

Pappy Broadway

School Bus Number 4 picked up Johnny, Becky, Nell Edith, Rosalie, Polly and me all the time,
It was the "end of the road bus," had one of the longest routes to make, and turned around at the county line.

It was an old bus, patched together over the years, slow, cumbersome, faded and outdated.
And it kinda matched its driver, an elderly man named Pappy Broadway, the slowest driver God ever created.

Pappy was tall and lean, and as far as we knew, our route had always been his trip.
He wore an old man's hat and overalls. I think pants would have slid down off his hips.

We were first on in the morning, last off at the end of each school day.
Some roads were paved, but we rode on gravel most of the way.

Down Dale Road, then up and back down Rock House Road, stopping every quarter mile or so.
Pappy zipped along on the gravel roads at a steady 18 mph, but on the main highway, he really let go.

He was no speed demon, and it took him a long time to make the drive.
My memory fails me, but I think one time on the speedometer, he actually hit thirty-five!!

Pappy also operated a little ice cream shop for the school out behind the gym.
And did odd jobs around the school, so wherever you were on campus, you might see him.

I think of Pappy now and then, his nod and smile, one of those unforgettable folks you meet along the way.
He drove us safely from home to school and back many years. But at 35 mph, it seemed like we were on that bus all day!

Rest in Peace, Pappy.

Curfew

On a Saturday night in the summer of nineteen hundred and sixty-one,
I stopped at the poolroom in town after taking Margaret, my future wife home.

She had to be home by ten, no matter what night we had a date.
I had to be home by midnight on weekends, no excuse for being late.

I was shooting pool, my eye on the clock and about eleven-thirty or so,
Terry, a friend, came in and said he bought a 1957 Chevy and did I want to go,

To the only straight stretch of road in the mountains to try it out and see what the car would do.
I looked at my watch, told Terry no, I would have to go home when my game was through.

You see, on Sunday morning, the whole family went to church in my car.
And to miss being home by midnight would be like me playing with fire.

I told Terry, reluctantly, not tonight, but I would catch up with him again.
But he would not be alone, because three other friends jumped in.

I got home about five minutes to twelve and immediately went to bed.
The 1957 Chevy hit the gas pumps doing over 120 at five after twelve, they said.

Two died in the fiery crash, my friend Terry and one other survived.
I credit God's protection, parents that cared, and the curfew for my being alive.

We raced cars, clocking how fast they would go, and I guess today that seems kind of lame.
But back in the mountains, back in the day, we looked at it more like a game.

Still, often I think of that night and what happened so long ago.
And I thank God for giving me the common sense and courage to say no.

Guilty, Your Honor

It was late summer of 1959, I was sixteen, happy, carefree, and leaving the football practice field,
When a patrolman caught me speeding as I went home on a stretch of road called Burleson Hill.

Not to worry, though, I thought as I looked at the cost and the court date when I would have to pay the fine.
I knew Judge Jack Tappan, a fan of the team, and had dated his daughter Mary once upon a time.

So, about a week before my court date and the fine of nearly twenty dollars was due,
I went to see Mr. Jack, who was cutting his lawn and drinking a brew or two.

He hugged me like a long-lost son, wanted to know how the team looked and if we could win it all this year.
I told him we could, and explained my ticket problem. He listened casually and had another beer.

Don't you worry, son, he said, anything for you boys on the team. Then he told me he would not be on the bench that day.
But I'll talk to my friend who is, he said. Plead guilty, he will suspend the fine, and you won't have to pay.

I show up in court, maybe three dollars in my pocket, at the appointed time.
The judge says, how do you plead? I said guilty, sir. He said that will be an eighteen-dollar fine.

I stumbled and fumbled, not knowing what to do.
Then in a low voice, I asked, didn't Judge Tappan talk to you?

What did you say, boy? The judge said as he looked down at me with nothing but contempt.
I mumbled nothing, sir; it's just that I did not come prepared to pay the fine, at least not all of it.

Young man, the judge said, you've got exactly one hour to pay the fine, or I will issue a warrant for your arrest.
Yes, sir, I said as I hurried away, my mind racing, not knowing what I was going to do next.

Now eighteen dollars to a sixteen-year-old in the summer of nineteen hundred and fifty-nine,
Would look like two or three hundred dollars to a teenager in this day and time.

You see, I had not told my parents about this because this was the second ticket that I had.
I got the first one the week I got my license for passing on a curve, and this would really make Dad mad.

A young man named Cotton ran a Shell station out on Grassy Creek, and to all teenagers, he was a friend.

I hurried out there, about three miles away, and told my friend Cotton the predicament I was in.

Without hesitation, he reached in the cash register and handed me a twenty-dollar bill.

I'll pay you back when I get my pay from the Big Lynn Lodge, I said. Cotton replied, I know you will.

I thanked him profusely, raced back, and paid my fine, getting there with about ten minutes to spare.

The folks never found out, I paid my friend back, and never had to pay another ticket there.

I guess the moral of this story is don't try to get a ticket taken care of with a judge that's drinking beer.

Because, at least in my case, ten minutes after I left, I doubt Judge Tappan remembered my being there.

Mistaken Identity

Someone asked me the other day if I had ever come face to face with a gun. I said I had a long time ago when I was about twenty-one.

I stopped to get gas at a station, not very far from home, in a town called Banner Elk.

I waited for someone to come out and help because back then you did not pump the gas yourself.

No one came out to help, so I got out and stood by the side of my car, wondering why.

That's when I saw this man, with a pistol, out of the corner of my eye.

With a loud mountain voice, he told me not to move and, "you stay right where you are at."

My legs were frozen, I couldn't run, or make a move to the car to get my trusty ball bat.

About ten feet away, he suddenly stopped; his puzzled look became a frown.
His countenance changed as he looked me over and slowly lowered the gun down.

I'm sorry he said, very softly as he tucked the pistol back in his belt.
It's a case of mistaken identity. You look just like somebody else.

I was trembling as I muttered something brilliant like "no harm done,"
jumped in the car, and got out of there fast.
I drove with my heart pounding and my hands shaking about five miles before realizing I still hadn't got any gas.

I don't know if the man with the gun found who he was looking for at a later date.
My prayer would be they reconciled, or he got out of town before it was too late.

In my seventy-six years on this earth, that time was the only one,
That I ever stared death in the face in front of an angry man with a gun.

I guess it's one of the reasons I don't carry today, although I understand why some people do.
If I make a mistake and your life I take, I can tell your family I'm sorry, but I can only weep for you.

Tempers, guns, and angry people seem to be in abundant supply.
So chill, let it go. It's not worth it, or you will be in jail, wondering why.

Stella

I think she was the first girl I ever had in the back seat of my 1952 Chevrolet.
I'm pretty sure it was a weekday night when we drove out to the Blue Ridge Parkway.

You see, her dad was a part-time preacher and worked away from home during the week.
He would only let her date in daylight hours, but her mother would "let her break that rule," so to speak.

To say she was wild would be putting it mildly because she was so restricted at home.
Wherever we were, on a date, at church or school, Stella would not leave me alone.

She became very possessive and wanted to dominate all of my time.
When I would try to break up, she would cry and mess with my mind.

She would call all hours of the day and night,
Telling me, she would have her brother beat me up in a fight.

Finally, I had enough and ended it for good one day.
I was afraid that to hold on to me, she would get in a family way.

However, one Sunday afternoon about a year later when I was feeling low,
I picked her up, and we drove to a remote spot off the parkway for another rendezvous.

Thankfully it was a one-time, last time thing.
We parted that day and never got together again.

I met my true love, got married, and we moved away from where we grew up and settled in Tennessee.
Stella married, settled in Spruce Pine, and I've had no contact with her, nor has she with me.

I've hesitated writing about her because a lot of what I could write would not be rated PG.
But I felt I should because, as in all of the poems about my life, I try to be as honest as I can be.

Shoot Again Sheriff

One hot night in June, Johnny's dad, Uncle Slim drove,
My dad, my cousin, Johnny, and me to a revival meeting at Chestnut Grove.

Chestnut Grove is a beautiful country Baptist Church in Little Switzerland, NC,
In the heart of the Blue Ridge Mountains, as scenic a place as you will ever see.

But at ages ten and nine, Johnny and I ran those hills and saw that beauty every day.
And rather than hear some preacher drone on and on, we would rather have stayed home and played.

But here we were on that hot night sitting several rows behind daddy and Uncle Slim.
An old man down from us started to go to sleep, and Johnny whispered, "Look at him."

The old man kept leaning, and I whispered, "He's going fast."
Then just before he fell over, he raised up and passed some gas!!

Well, we giggled rather softly, but enough to make our dads look around.
But we sat up straight, took on a solemn look, so all they did was frown.

But the old man wasn't through and as he again started to lean and sleep,
Another blast came out of his overalls as he shifted and swayed in his seat.

Well, it was tough to keep our composure, and for a moment, we were doing fine.
Then Johnny whispered to me, "He must have missed his target the first time."

That was it. We could not contain ourselves. Our laughter, along with the old man's fumes, now filled the air.
Daddy and Uncle Slim turned around, and their looks told us exactly what was going to happen when we got out of there.

Well, we got home, and I explained why we were laughing and what Johnny had said.
I got a good talking to, no whipping, and I thought I saw a smile on daddy's face as he sent me to bed.

I can't remember my cousin's fate, though I doubt his dad was as benevolent as mine.
The moral of this story is to be quiet, reverent, and attentive because watching old men will get you in trouble every time.

Blue Devils, Bulldogs, and the Sheriff

All four of my high school years, I played football for Harris High in Spruce Pine, NC.
Our biggest rival was Bakersville, and the hatred between us was there for all to see.

There was trouble every time we played, and the teams five years' probation had barely come to an end.
And before this night was over the two teams would be on probation and not play for five years again.

We were the Blue Devils, and the Bulldogs was their nickname.
It was a slobber knocking street fight every time we played a game.

And so, it was we went to their field in mid-season 1960, late in the fall.
Both teams undefeated, the Bulldogs had not been scored on at all.

The whole county attended, the place was electric, and several fights broke out.
Both teams had players ejected, but that's not what I want to tell you about.

Coach Norton called a time out; we huddled around him with less than a minute left to go.
Run to the gym dressing room in a group when the game ends, he said, hurry up and don't be slow.

We did and got dressed without the usual yelling after a win, sensing something was wrong.
Then we heard a brick shatter against the door, peeped out and saw the gym filled with a yelling throng.

We stayed in the dressing room listening to the mob outside, not knowing what we were going to do.
Then through the door came Sheriff Robinson and one deputy. The Sheriff said, "ok guys, line up two by two."

I know you've had a tough game, he said as he talked to us.
Now Deputy Burleson and I will walk you to the bus.

I looked at my friend Don Ray, and he looked back at me.
We were going to be the first two out but moved back to number three.

The Sheriff opened the door to a gym full of yelling, screaming people cursing at us.
Calmly he looked around and said, "get behind me, gentlemen, we are going to the bus."

As we stepped out, a 300-pound redneck yelled something, and to this day, I don't know what he said in his shout.
What I do know is from nowhere came a slapjack in the hand of the Sheriff, and teeth flew out of the redneck's mouth.

Bring him, Sheriff Robinson said and helped the Deputy scoop the big man off the gymnasium floor.
The crowd was so quiet you could have heard a mouse pee on cotton as we hurried out the door.

I learned a valuable lesson that night, one that has served me well time and time again.
Never, ever mouth off to a small in stature Sheriff, especially if he has a slapjack in his hand.

Friday Night Lights

As I grow older, my mind wanders back through the years,
To a timeless hurried, no worries or fears.

I remember a crisp Friday night; Harris High Blue Devils was our team's name.
Tough old mountain boys, football was our game.

We would run out on the field to the cheers and bright lights,
My future wife in the stands as the band played "Oh What A Night."

There were Jack and Clayton, Davis, Jerry, Billy H., and Billy G.,
Johnny, Mike, Don Ray and Bobby, Danny, Lawrence, Larry, and me.

We took on all comers, Coach John Norton, our boss.
Never got a state championship, but we won more than we lost.

Life happens; time passes faster than the games we play.
Four quick years of football and high school and its graduation day.

Some got married, some moved away, and some stayed in town.
Some went to college; others got jobs; some went to Vietnam.

Many years have passed, fall, football, and October are near.
Outside my window I see the leaves falling, winter will soon be here.

I think of how wonderful God has been to me, all the ways I've been blessed.
Great wife, sons, and grandson, much more than I could ever ask.

Had a great job, made a profitable living, traveled this earth to its ends.
Have been blessed with restorative health, a few possessions, and plenty of trustworthy friends.

Still, as I look out the window in the twilight of life much more than fortune or fame,
I wish I could go back to October 1960, and play in just one more game.

The Play

In my Junior year at Harris High School, I decided to try out for the Junior play.
I had no acting experience, and if I had been called a thespian, someone would dearly pay.

"Papa Was A Preacher" was the title, and I thought maybe I would get a bit part to do.
It might help me meet some girls, and maybe play practice would get me out of a class or two.

To my surprise, I was cast as Papa, an older pastor trying to keep his family in line.
Talk about miscasting!! No one would have ever mistaken me for a preacher, then or anytime.

Opposite me as my wife was a young lady named Sara I had known since we started the first grade.
Had it not been for her help and encouragement, not even a TV minister would I have made.

I remember Dickie, Julia, Danny, Bill, Phillip, Peggy, and others were in the play.
And Mrs. Bryant, our director, must have thought we would never be ready for opening day.

We had a lot of fun rehearsing, and Sara and I played off each other very well.
Except the time I, the preacher, answered the phone and said, "oh hell!!"

The play went off without a hitch, and we did three or four performances at night and for the kids in school.
I credit "Mama" as I called Sara in the play, with helping me get all my lines down and keeping my cool.

We ran in different circles then, my costar and me.
After the play, I thought we might hook up, but it was not to be.

Still, we were "married" for the duration of the play as we raised a family,
So, God bless you, "Mama," classmate and friend. You are an unforgettable castmate to me.

The Smoking Corner

This is going to be hard for some of you folks to believe out there in the crowd,
But in the late fifties and sixties in Harris High School, Spruce Pine NC, smoking was allowed.

Yep, by any measure of thinking, this policy was nuts.
But bringing a note from parents let you smoke them butts.

The designated smoking area was outside in a corner where the buildings met.
And I've seen forty smoking at a time in sunshine, snow, and in rain soaking wet.

That sort of thing would indeed be reported and frowned on today.
But back then, several schools in NC allowed it, thinking smoking was ok.

Now I can hear you asking if I ever frequented the smoking corner since I said I would be honest in all I wrote.
Yes, I did, but not very often. Bummed a cigarette now and then, and no one ever asked to see a note.

"Smoke'em if you've got'em." (Cough)

Petticoat Malfunction

It was in the spring of 1959; I don't remember the exact date,
That I went to the rink on Friday night because I loved to skate.

I was skating to the music, popping the whip, working up a sweat,
When I bumped into my friend Don, and a beautiful girl he had just met.

He took me aside and asked to borrow my car to take his new friend home.
He said his car was in the shop and he wouldn't be gone long.

I tossed him my keys and told him to hurry.
It was nine o'clock then, and I had to be home by ten-thirty.

Now that part of the story ended that Friday night,
But Saturday morning was when the problem came to light.

As sure as Saturday morning came around,
I would take Mama, Grandpa, and sister Polly into town.

As I was helping Grandpa get in the car's front seat,
Mama opened the back door and let out a shriek.

I left Grandpa and ran around to the back door.
A black petticoat and a pair of panties were lying on the seat and floor.

I told Mama I knew nothing about those, again, and again I would repeat.
Mama yelled, this is certainly your car, and this is your back seat.

I mumbled and protested, but it didn't matter what I said.
By this time, Mama's hair wasn't her only feature that was red.

As we drove to town, Mama told me over and over about my sinning.
My sister Polly looked puzzled, and Grandpa kept grinning.

Just when I thought Mama's tirade would never end,
She became quite and never mentioned the incident again.

So, I guess the moral of this story is if you loan your car to a friend,
Check out the back seat before anyone gets back in.

The Girl on the Bus

Another experience I debated about putting on paper, one that does not show yours truly in the best of light.
But if I'm going, to be honest about my life, and I am, then I have to tell you what happened on the bus that night.

I had worked the summer in Wisconsin, made enough money in a poker game to buy a bus ticket home.
I boarded the bus in Milwaukee, had a two-hour layover in Chicago, with many more stops to come.

I got on the bus in Chicago at eleven pm, walked nearly to the back, and took a window seat.
I saw her get on, look up and down the rows, then lost track of her as I put my small bag under my feet.

Suddenly she sat down beside me. Startled, I looked at her, and she smiled.
As she settled in, she said looks like you and I are going to be together for a while.

She was a sophomore in college, she said, and that she was on her way to Ohio.
The University of Cincinnati, she grinned so we will be seatmates for at least six hours or so.

By this time, we were rolling, and soon we were out of the city, and the bus was dark and quiet.
I thought she was asleep as she kind of fell over against me as we rolled on through the night.

Then I felt her hand going on a journey only she could want it to take.
And when she turned her lips up to mine, I knew there was no mistake.

She produced a blanket from somewhere that covered us up to our neck.
I kept looking around, thinking someone could see us and start raising heck.

She said don't worry about it, so what if someone sees us, what are they going to say?
Nobody cares; no one is watching, and it's none of their business anyway.

Well, the girl had a point I thought as I eased back in my seat and began to settle down inside.
I became calm and relaxed, as best I could. She smiled and said, enjoy the ride.

And what a ride it was! As the countryside rolled by in the darkness, I lost all track of time and space.
When we finally stopped in Indy, I felt as if I had run a marathon or just finished a long, long race.

At Indianapolis, and we got off (thank goodness), used the restroom, then got back on the bus.
And she started right back where she left off with her under the blanket, then me, then both of us.

From Indy to Cincy, the trip was both too short and too long.
While I didn't want it to end, my strength was almost totally gone.

For her, it was the end of the line, her college town; for me, a change of bus was due.
She kissed my cheek, waved goodbye, and said it was nice riding with you.

I have no explanation why, of all the others on the bus, she came and sat down by me.
But it was the sixties after all when everything was supposed to be laid back, open, and free.

Some will say ET, you are fantasizing and tripping in your old age, but I am not at that point yet.
The exact times, dates, and stops in my mind are hazy, but what happened on that bus, I will never forget.

It's not something I'm proud of, hard to believe, and somewhat strange.
But on that long bus ride together, we never got each other's names.

Football and Life

In the fall of 1958, my football career began.
During the next four years, I played center, guard, and end.

Football is both simple and complex; some plays are old, and some are new.
But boil it down to its basic form, it's beating the man across from you.

One learns the team concept, each player separate, yet part of the whole,
Working in unison as they march down the field toward the goal.

I remember our coach, a firm disciplinarian, very old school in every way.
And his words, regimen, and life lessons are all a part of who I am today.

Guys, he would say as we knelt after a practice long and rough,
This ain't nothing you all, it's life beyond high school that's tough.

When you are out in the world, and life knocks you around,
You've tried and tried, but you are face down on the ground,

Reach deep down in your soul, remember this day and how you felt.
Then get up off your ass and get back in the game, you still have something left.

His words may have been crude, but there's no denying their truth.
I know because I've applied them many times since my youth.

Some say football is just a brutal, rugged game with no lessons you can take to the bank.
I beg to differ. I found out from a hard-line, old-time coach that you always have something left in the tank.

One Little Mistake

My good friend Larry and I never disagree on much as a rule,
But there is one little thing I keep hearing about when we played football in high school.

Now I'm going to tell you exactly what happened though he may disagree.
It happened as we played our arch-rival, the Bulldogs in Bakersville, NC.

We played for the Harris High Blue Devils. I was the center, and Larry played end.
He was also the punter, and every punt he ever kicked, I long snapped to my friend.

Now if he is honest as he relates this story to you,
Every snap up until and after that night was fast, chest high, and true.

But I made one little bitty mistake that night, my fault, no doubt.
But fifty years later, at reunions, it's all I still hear about.

The night I almost got him killed, he says with great emotion and strife.
That the first time, we had to punt, I dribbled the ball back to him, nearly costing him his life.

Now I don't remember it that way at all and let me tell you why.
First, I had to block the man right over me, and he was a great big ugly guy.

I still managed to center the ball and send it on its way.
But it bounced once and hit Larry right in the hands, no dribble like you say.

Still, he caught it, ran for a first down, and as I lay on my back, I could see.
But oh, no!! A flag was thrown, and the penalty was on me.

It seems I had "accidentally" grabbed the face mask of the big ugly man I had to block.

He never gave me any more trouble though, we won the game and ran out the clock.

So, in September, our Class of 1961 will gather for Reunion time again,
And once more, Larry will tell the sad tale of how I almost did him in.

Now, this is all in fun, you know, Larry and I are close friends, almost like brothers in every way.
But there is a life lesson to be learned here, something to be used each day.

No matter how much you practice, you are going to make mistakes.
It depends on how you adjust to them, the corrections that you make.

Therefore, be remembered for the good snaps, not the bobbles that you make.
Be known as a truly moral and Godly person, for in that there is no mistake.

The Center

He is the most overlooked and under-appreciated player on the football team.
That is until he messes up, and then he is the object of name-calling and screams.

He is the center, the guy in the middle, the first of the offensive team to hunker down.
The initial one to touch the ball, the one that every play revolves around.

He makes the calls for the offensive line, snaps for punts, field goals, and extra points after a score.
Deals with the shotgun, and sometimes a new QB with a case of nerves from the crowd's roar.

Then too, what every center knows but you will never hear him explain,
The adjustment to the way each QB's hands feel on your backside in a game.

He knows his primary job is to get the ball to the QB, punter, or holder each time.
And then take care of that big old ugly linebacker snarling at him from the other side of the line.

He labors in obscurity, this indispensable center, a vital but forgotten man in any football game.
But let him center the ball over the quarterback's head, and the whole world will know his name.

The Pile

Who doesn't love football? Most folks have been watching games for quite a while.
But unless and until you have played the game, you don't know what goes on in The Pile.

My descriptions cannot provide the smells, the sound of popping bones, the things that are said.
Or how it feels to have a couple thousand pounds of stinking guys laying on your head.

Alas, the trash-talking would make the most foul-mouthed person ask forgiveness for their sin.
Ancestry is questioned, and it goes way beyond ("how's your mama and them")

And the stench, at the bottom of The Pile, is almost too much to bear.
I don't think one old boy from Bakersville had bathed since we played last year!

But that's not the worst thing that can happen with your body wedged in a tight space.
Think about when a three hundred pounder farts right in your face.

Body parts are grabbed, pinched, pulled, and kicked.
You would like to eyeball who the culprit was, but in The Pile, you can't see a lick.

And Heaven help you if you recover a fumble because in your hands you have the prize!!
All I have described is now merely child's play as the punishment now intensifies.

But you hold on; the game is over, the victory has been won!
You hug and shake hands with your opponents and tell them you had fun.

The fans leave happy, savoring the first victory in quite a while.
Never knowing, not really caring, what went on in The Pile.

Ice Water Toting in Hell (Fall, 1960)

Our football team, the Harris High Blue Devils, came down from the mountains of Spruce Pine.
To play our nemesis in the valley, the rugged team called the Green Wave from Glen Alpine.

As we gathered our stuff, my cousin, Johnny, and I started the long walk to the gym.
Suddenly we were joined by this pint-sized foul-mouthed local kid, maybe nine or ten.

Hey, he said, lookin' at the H on our jackets, I bet that H stands for the Hills!!
Ain't much daylight up in them mountains, he continued. I'll bet coming down here is a thrill!!

Get lost kid, I said. Quit bothering us and get out of the way.
He didn't shut up, laughed, and said you will get your ass beat today.

Then again, he said that H stands for the Hills, and that's what I will always say.
Johnny said no, it stands for Hell, and that's where I'm going to kick you if you don't get out of the way.

Undeterred, the kid said, oh, I've been there so many times I've lost track.
The devil makes me tote ice water every time before he sends me back.

The kid ran off, leaving us laughing, and we never saw him anymore.
We beat Glen Alpine that night, not by much, but I don't remember the score.

I do remember that half-pint kid and his mouthy tongue as well.
And how he took an H and connected it to Harris, the Hills and toting water in Hell.

Finger Lickin' Good

(A true story not for the faint-hearted)

It was a beautiful fall in the mountains around the first of October,
Johnny, Larry, Tommy, Don Ray, and I went to a fair a few counties over.

We took in a strip show, rode the Ferris wheel, and swings,
Played some games on the midway, ate some cotton candy, and a few other things.

Then Don Ray yelled, "here's something we haven't seen."
The sign said, "Come and see Myrtle Eat a Live Chicken."

Looking back, I don't know what we were thinking.
I can't recall now, but we had probably been drinking.

We paid our twenty-five cents and walked into the tent,
Where an Amazon woman sat with snakes crawling around her in a pit.

The tent filled up quickly, and then the spectacle began.
And in the pit with the snakes and Myrtle sat a Rhode Island hen.

Myrtle yelled out a blood-curdling scream that would wake up the dead,
Grabbed that poor chicken and bit off its head.

I turned to my buddies, but only Johnny and Tommy were there.
Larry and Don Ray had both left this nightmare.

I looked back at Myrtle who now had blood running down her face,
Feathers and other parts of chicken flying all over the place.

Johnny looked at me, and we both were about to throw up.
By this time, Myrtle was already into the guts.

That ended our night at the Burke County Fair.

We ran out of that tent into the fresh mountain night air.
Five tough old mountain football players, never afraid of a fight,
Fled Myrtles tent trying to keep down what we had eaten that night.

Now when I pass a KFC with its sign, "Finger Lickin',"
I try not to think of the night we saw Myrtle eat a live chicken.

CHAPTER 7

Life Just Became Complicated

As the Statler Brothers so aptly sung in their song "The Class of 57 Had Its Dream," life gets complicated when you get past eighteen. In this chapter, you meet my immediate family and a bit of our history.

Margaret Willis Biddix

As I write this, it's been close to sixty years since we first met,
At Harris High School, it was a day I will never forget.

You were the most beautiful girl I had ever seen,
Someone, I thought only existed in my dreams.

Long black hair, beautiful complexion, and an hourglass figure to match.
Wow, I thought to myself, that lady would be quite a catch.

So, we talked for a while and got acquainted,
And for the rest of our high school years, we dated.

After high school, you soon became my wife,
And we began our journey together for the rest of our life.

We've traveled many roads since our journey began,
You have been my partner, lover, my very best friend.

It's not all been easy, many difficulties we have faced.
But we have always had each other and depended on God's Grace.

We had to move many times if, in my job with American Airlines, I was to remain.
You handled each move like a pro, never once did I hear you complain.

Two sons, a grandson, daughters in law and girlfriends have joined our family over the years.
You embrace them, love them, feed them, and they know they are always welcome here.

Your love for all of us has no end and will forever go on,
You are the rock of our family, the one we all lean on.

For me, you are all any man could wish for in a wife.
You are the perfect soulmate; in four words, you are my life.

Just as you did long ago on that memorable day,
When you enter the room, you still take my breath away.

I LOVE YOU.

Tommy Aaron Biddix

Our firstborn son, Tommy, came into this world on September 21, 1966.
Driving in a rainstorm, we could hardly see where we were going; it was so thick.

We made it to the Fairfax Virginia Hospital, around two am, in spite of the storm.
And around five to six hours later, Tommy Aaron Biddix was born.

I remember holding him carefully for the first time as he looked up at me,
And thinking of my responsibility to teach and care for him at my young age of twenty-three.

From that moment until today, life for Margaret and me has been filled with laughter and fun.
There have been ups and downs, but we have always pointed with pride to our firstborn son.

A skillful athlete, Tommy was known for how hard he practiced and played.
A total team player, never selfish, led by example, one of his coaches said.

A conscientious student, he managed to work part-time and keep his grades up as well.
He had a memory for events happening, as he grew up, even down to the smallest detail.

Soft-spoken, a pleasant demeanor, and courteous to everyone that he meets,
You would never know that once he gets angry, a raging temper lies beneath.

Now. I don't mean that his temper is quick or bad.
It takes a lot of time and provoking to get him really mad.

But when his temper flares, the earth moves, so, one had best get out of his way.
He is ready for action, saying in very pointed words what he has to say.

We were very proud when Tommy went to college and graduated at
MTSU.
He is the only one in Margaret's or my family to make it all the way through.

A good citizen and family man, hard worker, respected by everyone,
Tommy has been a good teacher, friend, and father to Aaron, our grandson.

As we approach our sunset, we look back at the many right and wrong things we have done.
But one thing is sure, and time has proven, we could never ask for a better son.

So, enjoy your birthday with family and friends, the laughter and the cheers.
And may God bless you and give you good health and happiness for another fifty years.

Bobby Travis Biddix

I had just gotten home from my job with American Airlines, April 10, 1968,
It was well after midnight, so the hour was very late.

My wife Margaret was up, very pregnant, and as she spoke,
She said we'd better get to the hospital, my water just broke.

Tommy was 18 months old, and we got him ready,
And headed to Baptist Hospital in our 1967 red Chevy.

A curfew was in place because of the assignation of Dr. Martin Luther King,
But thankfully, nothing hindered us, not barricades, policemen, or anything.

Around five that morning, our second son was born, Bobby Travis, his name.
And I can tell you our lives, in a fantastic way, have never been the same.

Bobby was always his own person, went his own way, living life to the limit.
He could have excelled as a baseball or basketball player, but his heart was never really in it.

He never seemed to care for team or organized sports,
It was bicycles, skateboards, motorcycles, and things of that sort.

Fifty-one years have passed since that night in Nashville long ago,
Over the years, through the ups and downs, we've watched Bob grow.

There are many places he's been, accomplishments he has done,
Caving, mountain climbing, bicycling, author, many awards won.

All these things make us proud of you, and we always will be,
But thank you most for the love and respect you've shown to your Mother and me.

As our sunset approaches, we look back on our life's work, family, and things we might have done.
But there is one thing never in question: We could not have had a better son.

So, God bless you on your birthday and despite our parental anxiety, worry, and fears,
May He grant you safety and health to continue your adventurous spirit for another fifty years.

Aaron Morgan Biddix

Out of all of my writings, I've never written exclusively about my grandson Aaron, until now.
So, for want of a better term, it is time to cut to the chase, where my prior writings did not allow

Aaron Morgan Biddix was born February 22, 1996, on a cold, overcast winter day.
Weighing just over three pounds and two months premature, tubes were running in and out of his toy-like body every which way.

Delivered by cesarean, when I first saw him, not a mark on his tiny body could be found.
But, I thought, as I looked at him. What kind of a chance does he have at only three pounds?

Then one of those exceptional nurses said something that is still fresh in my mind.
He's a fighter she said, his heartbeat is strong, vitals are good, he'll do just fine.

Well, I did not feel that way, and the story is told in the poem *Thank God for Unanswered Prayers*.
However, Aaron got along fine, no extended problems, and in just over a month he was out of there

The formative years from one until six were some of the best Margaret and I spent with our only grandson.
Playing in the leaves, with Rocky, our dog, throwing and catching balls, outings, or picnics, we always had plenty of fun.

But as Aaron started playing organized sports, we began to see what exceptional abilities he had.
Baseball was his main sport; he could play any position, fast as a hiccup, an attitude that made any coaches heart glad.

He played guard in youth basketball, excelled in running and soccer too.
But as he entered middle school, he was still waiting for that growth spurt that was overdue.

While he excelled in tryouts for the Siegel Middle School baseball team,
His relatively small size caused him to refocus his dreams.

Undeterred, he went out for the Tennis Team and the Bowling Team too.
And he played and starred on both until his high school days were through.

We've played golf together, and he always wins when we go.
He has had two, maybe three perfect games in bowling, I know.

Going to the Titans games for many years with Aaron and his dad,
Provided us with a lot of bonding and some of the best times we ever had.

Aaron has always had a good head on his shoulders, even-tempered, and did well in school.
Likable, never met a stranger, respectful to all he meets, and practices the Golden Rule.

He will definitely be in line for a management position in any field he wants to be.
Aaron will graduate in the fall with a business degree from Middle Tennessee.

So, if Memaw and Pa seem incredibly proud of our grandson, it's because we are.
We love him, wish him the best, and with God's hand in his, Aaron will go far.

We love you,

FBI

During the Vietnam War build-up, I was not drafted and have often wondered why.
It may have been because, during that war, I worked for the FBI.

I was a young twenty-year-old in January of 1963,
When we left home and moved to an apartment in southeast Washington, DC.

For the next four years, I worked in the Files and Communications Division of the FBI.
My wife's application was approved, and she came to work in the same division in July.

We were serving our country and, in our work, seeing the good and the bad as part of the staff.
We were granted the highest security clearance a civilian could have.

We witnessed a lot of the nation's history in our four-years run,
John Glenn's parade, Kennedy's assassination, and The March on Washington.

We saw the sights and visited the many shrines and monuments to be found.
We even saw the Mona Lisa at the National Art Gallery downtown.

We became accustomed to each other during these early years in DC.
Working, loving, sharing, learning, no worries about what was to be.

But life has its ways of moving on and getting our attention.
We were starting a family, and at the FBI, the only advancement was by attrition.

So, with Margaret being pregnant, I took the best option at the time,
And began what turned out to be a thirty-seven-year career with American Airlines.

We have never regretted those early days working for the FBI in Washington, DC.
It helped form who we are, our value system, our love of country, each other, and what it means to be free.

1964 Chevelle

In 1964 I turned twenty-one which meant I could now do what I hadn't been able to do yet,
What every red-blooded American does, buy a car, and go in debt.

And what a car it was!! Though it was over fifty years ago, it seems like only yesterday,
That I went to the dealer and picked up the first-year model of the Chevelle Chevrolet.

It had bucket seats, a four-barrel carb, 283 cubic engine, four in the floor, and the color was Daytona Blue.
And that sucker would run, gave the Mopars a run for their money, back in the day, and that wasn't easy to do.

I was driving home from working at the airport one Sunday night when a Dodge pulled up beside me at a light.
He had drag numbers on his windshield, he looked at me, I nodded, and we took off into the night.

Now my Chevelle had the meanest second gear of any car I had ever seen.
And I was in second gear and about four car lengths ahead of him not long after the light turned green.

I guess I held in second up to about ninety, as long as I could.
When I hit third gear, the Mopar drove by me, as I was pretty sure he would.

We stopped about two miles down the road, and he got out, shaking his head, looking at me with a grin.
I thought you were going to blow me away; he said, what in the world have you got in that thing??

I smiled and said everything is stock, no modification, or anything.
There is one thing though, I told him. It's got the meanest second gear I've ever seen.

I knew I would take you at the start and would be ahead till I had to hit third gear.
That's when I knew you would pass me. You did, and we came on up and stopped here.

We talked cars for a while, shook hands, and I drove away into the night and home.
But that Chevelle was a great ride, the first one I ever bought and the fastest car I ever owned.

Aaron's Eyes

Aaron's eyes met mine as he walked to the plate.
The game was tied, the inning was late.

Then I heard the crack of the bat, and the ball went past a diving shortstop who fell on his face.
Aaron rounded first, never slowing down and slid safely into second base.

That he scored the winning run to me came as no surprise,
For I could see it in his eyes.

Double-A

Our grandson, Aaron, played little league baseball beginning at age nine.
Since Margaret and I were retired, we were able to see his games most of the time.

Now Aaron was, and is, a good player no matter the position.
Second, third, short, outfield, catcher, he could always make the transition.

He loved to pitch, had good control but was not very fast.
He got to pitch some, but only if other pitchers were used, and he was the last.

I was working Disaster Relief in New Orleans during the Katrina clean up, rebuild and all,
And missed one of the games when Aaron got the call.

My son, Tommy, said it was the best game you could ever hope to see.
And when it was over, Aaron's team had won by a score of five to three.

Aaron pitched the entire game and when checking the scorebook after the game was done,
They discovered something that rarely happens in Little League: he had not walked anyone.

When I got home, I told him how I hated not seeing him pitch in the game.
Aaron looked at me kind of funny and said Pa; you were there with me just the same.

I looked at him intently and asked him to explain what he said.
Oh, I didn't mean in person, you were there in my head.

When I got in a jam in my mind, I could hear you say,
"Come on, bear down, you can do it Double-A."

Aaron said in all of the noise and cheers I hear from those that watch us play,
You are the only one in the stands that ever calls me Double-A.

His Memaw called him into the kitchen before I could speak.
And I'm glad she did so he didn't see the tears roll down my cheeks.

Rocky

He was not our dog in the beginning when he came from Texas with Bob, our son.
But Bob moved into an apartment, and Rocky, a chocolate Chow, came to live in our home.

He was not a big dog as Chows go, weighing about forty-eight pounds when he was grown.
He lived to be nearly seventeen years old, and we thank God for each one.

He was a good watchdog, gentle but very protective, especially of Margaret, my wife.
He would sleep at the foot of her bed when I was on the road, protecting her with his life.

We took three-mile walks together nearly every day.
What a workout that was with Rocky pulling hard all the way.

It always amazed me how Rocky knew the perimeter of our home.
And as soon as someone stepped on the property, his bark let you know a visitor had come.

Then one day, a stranger came in the form of a baby, Aaron, our Grandson.
And I guess Rocky was jealous that the attention was now on another one.

For a long time, he would whine, pout, and bark when Aaron came into view.
Then one day, it was if he said everyone likes him, I guess I will too.

So, they became great buddies, and they would tumble and play.
Although we trusted Rocky not to hurt Aaron, one of us was never far away.

The years passed, as they tend to do.
Rocky and I got older, and our walks got shorter too.

Then after several visits to the kind vet, he put his hand on my shoulder and said no more could be done.
Monday, he would euthanize him, and I could take him home for the weekend, his last one.

Rocky loved cheese, so I went to the grocery store and bought some of the best.
And every time I thought of it, I would give him a slice, and on Monday I gave him the rest.

I brought him back from the vet in a quilt and buried him in the back yard where he liked to roam.
It was July, and sweat was not the only drops falling from my face as I dug his final home.

Dogs in Heaven? I don't know. I've got too much to worry about in the here and now.
But if there are, I know one thing for sure—Heaven just got a little brighter with Rocky, the beautiful Chow.

Coach Ed

I was having lunch with a good friend in Murfreesboro the other day,
And as we often do, we lamented how society seems to have lost its way.

Take sports for kids, my friend said, as we ordered the meal of the day.
Nowadays, even if they lose every kid gets a trophy anyway.

The thought crossed my mind; there are a lot more pressing problems today than that.
But I was very thoughtful and careful in what I said as I answered him back.

I said, well, I coached kids ages nine through thirteen in baseball and basketball for ten years or so.
We won more than we lost, had a world of fun, a championship or two, and helped the players grow.

But the thing that troubled me then and still weighs heavily on my heart,
Are the kid's situation(s) when you meet them for the first time, and practice starts.

Let's say you have fifteen players on your roster to call on the phone.
It's a safe bet you won't have five with both parents living at home.

Divorce, drugs, some parents are in jail, others don't care.
absent mothers and fathers, gone, and no one knows where.

But my friend, the saddest situations, hardest to take the very worst of all,
Are those that take physical and verbal abuse, and are made to feel small.

So, there they stand before you, most hoping for a break from the daily despair.
Some wanting to learn, many made to come, others don't care.

I, and the coaches that helped me, always started the year off with the same theme.
Love them, teach them the game, be sure that each one knows how important they are to the team.

Rules were few and simple. No talking back to coaches or referees, this rule you don't want to test.
Be at the practices and games on time, and most important of all, DO YOUR BEST.

One thing that was important to me then and would be a deal-breaker if I coached today.
I would never coach in any league where ALL THE KIDS on the roster did not get to play.

You took them, coached them, loved them, molded them, and then right before your eyes,
Individuals became a team, problems at home forgotten, on the field nothing but blue skies.

Many times, after a tough loss and in silence, the team gathered around, heads hanging down.
Did you do your best? I asked. They would nod. Then walk proudly and get your heads off the ground.

When you win, celebration, losing brings misery and strife.
That's when you console and teach them it's all a part of life.

Trophies? Yeah, we gave one to everyone when the season was done.
But by then, they had earned it with hard work, not just games won.

I greatly miss that part of my life, but occasionally something happens that gladdens my heart.
A former player now grown will tell me, Mr. Biddix, thank you. I owe you because in my life you played a big part

My Son Can Pitch??

As our sons were growing up in the seventies, I spent about ten years coaching Little League Baseball,
It was a great time in my life. A time of enjoying teaching and learning, I wouldn't take anything for at all.

Funny though, as I look back on it now how all the parents thought their child could pitch.
So, in this brief missive, I will try to relate how one day I scratched that itch.

It was a makeup game sometime in June, about 98 degrees in the heat of the day.
There was some discussion with the board because it was so hot, but they decided we could play.

We covered the dugout with a tarp, had plenty of water and wet towels to wipe away the sweat.
My problem was I had used my best time pitchers, they were on rest and not eligible to pitch yet.

As the home team, we took the field, and that's when the trouble began.
The little left-hander I had on the mound was walking batters again, again, and again.

So I brought in my left fielder, a big boy, sturdy and stout.
Seven batters later, I strode once again to the mound because he hadn't got a single out.

So I brought in my first basemen, and right away, he removed all doubt.
Low and behold on just eight pitches, he managed to get the first out.

He then gave up five more runs as he began to loosen his stuff.
The score read thirteen to zero when I told him that was enough.

You get the gist of what was happening, in that heat, what we were going through.
We did get three outs. They let us bat then called the game, and we never played inning two.

I looked at the scoreboard, thirty to nothing, as we walked off the field feeling bad.
But not another time that year did I hear "let my kid pitch" because l "pitched" every player I had.

CHAPTER 8

Some Facts, Some Opinions

Opinions: Like noses, we've all got'em. (Better not give you the country version of that old saying). This chapter contains my thoughts on a variety of subjects, as well as some indisputable facts. A few will make you smile. Many, I hope, will cause considerable thought and maybe initiate an action or two.

Opinions

Opinions are like noses we all have one. This old saying relates that sentiment is very clear.
There is a more expressive old country form of this saying, but I can't say it here.

Our Constitution gives us the right to speak up and give our opinion here in the land of the free.
But it seems like in these turbulent times we are living in everyone is giving their opinions to ME!

So, here's a suggestion for folks from whom I get an unsolicited opinion every time they speak:
Get on your cellphone or computer, rave and rant all you want, but do it in a silent TWEET.

Memorial Day

Today is Memorial Day. The first holiday of the warm weather season.
I wonder, as we celebrate, how many folks pause to remember the reason.

Today is Memorial Day. Families on the lake and golf course, engaged in many types of play.
Perhaps never giving a thought to those that gave their life so we all could enjoy this day.

Today is Memorial Day. How many children have grown up not knowing Mother or Dad?
Because they fell in some foreign land, spilling the last drop of blood they had.

Today is Memorial Day. I thank God for everyone that served and all they went through.
But mainly, I give thanks for those that soon will be gone, the veterans of World War Two.

Today is Memorial Day. Find someone who served, thank them, and shake their hand.
The sacrifices of those living and gone are the reason we enjoy the bounty of this great land.

Today is Memorial Day. As we enjoy family, food, and friends may we not forget to bow and pray,
Thanking God for His many blessings on this nation that continually come our way.

Today is Memorial Day. As we think of those who serve, have served, and all they have been through,
I pray our leaders and the citizens of our nation will realize we need to turn to You.

Today is Memorial Day. May we also pray God will be with each one serving and their families wherever they are.
God bless the memory of those who have died, the loved ones left behind, and we pray there will be no more war.

TODAY IS MEMORIAL DAY

Majestic Oak

Mighty and proud over two centuries she stood for everyone to see
On the Stones River Civil War Battlefield in Murfreesboro, Tennessee.

Many folks had rested under her branches in the shade,
Spending time with families, playing, picnicking, and drinking lemonade.

Never stopping to think what the old oak had seen and withstood,
Years ago, young men from the North and South soaked the grass around her with their sweat and their blood.

Yet she withstood the fighting, losing a few branches with cannonballs landing.
The twenty-first century saw her tall and still standing.

A powerful tornado hit Murfreesboro on April 10, 2009, spreading devastation all around.
The Majestic Oak swayed in the wind, roots straining and popping until she toppled to the ground.

It was just a tree, some folks might say,
Cut it up, use it for firewood, get it out of the way.

But the old tree was a significant landmark of history, and she had seen it all, stood tall, stayed the same.
We lost a piece of Americana that day, a part we can never reclaim.

Worry

It seems humans are prone to worry a lot,
About this and that, and sometimes we don't even know what.

Worries about the future, today, and yesterday,
Trouble in our minds that will not go away.

We worry about our jobs, our families, and our health.
Or if the stock market crashes, taking away all our wealth.

Should I buy a new car or maybe build a swimming pool?
And how do I pay for the kid's college after high school?

So, what should we do when the worries of life come each day?
Use your best judgment on each situation, and pray.

And remember through it all, what statistics say,
Only twenty percent of what we worry about ever happens anyway.

Children in Cages

Terrible things often happen, things that are cruel, degrading, and vile.
Among the worst offenders are those that would harm older people or a child.

In our country today, the battle over illegal immigration rages.
But never would I have believed my country would put children in cages.

Most of those struggling to get here are escaping drug lords, poverty, and strife.
Only a few are gang members or criminals; most want a better life.

Under the current administration separating families is the policy in use.
They are tearing small children away from their parent's loving arms, accepting no excuse.

I cannot imagine being there, the anguish, the crying, the pain.
Parents and children wondering if they will ever see each other again.

I can't do anything about it except pray and wonder why.
And when praying, I try to imagine what it must be like, and I begin to cry.

God, why does this country that I love do such a terrible thing to others?
Don't You tell us, in the Bible, we are supposed to love one another?

And where are the Christian people Lord, the ones that always raise such an enormous outcry?
About every life being precious. They are so quiet, and I have to wonder why???

But thankfully, I know where You are God, and it's not with the heartless politicians that gave the order.
You are with the broken hearts, comforting, and holding the hands of children in cages at the border.

Prejudice

What a terrible, terrible thing it is to have hatred in your heart,
And suppress that disdain for your fellowman until it tears your soul apart.

Though it breaks my heart, I have more respect for the woman or the man,
That does not try to hide their feelings, and I know exactly where they stand.

Then you have the folks that go on, and you think they will never shut up.
Telling you over and over, how they are not prejudiced—-but,

Then they usually begin a tirade on all the things they are upset about, immigrants, this and that.
And it always ends the same old way, "those people," which means people of color, but mainly those that are black.

God must look down with a heavy heart on this our nation,
And shed a tear when He sees how some are treating others in His creation.

So, let's stop the hate, and start loving each other,
Because in God's eyes, we are all sisters and brothers.

Fading Away

There is a select group of very distinguished Americans among us today,
Whose numbers are rapidly diminishing and slowly fading away.

These men and women saved this nation for me and you.
I am talking about a group that soon will be gone, the Veterans of World War Two.

According to the Department of Veterans Affairs in September of last year,
There are under four hundred thousand of these hero's still here.

I hope the young people will honor and preserve these Veterans memory, and the price they had to pay,
And realize the Greatest Generation is the reason we are not speaking German and Japanese today.

Most of these Veterans are now well into their nineties, and soon, the last one will pass away.
So, if you are fortunate enough to know these extraordinary Americans, thank them without delay.

A divided America needs hero's now probably more than we ever will
Surely, we can all agree these men and women more than fit the bill.

Let's thank God for these aging Veterans from the mountains, cities, and rural valleys of every State.
Hug them, love them, thank them, and help them in any way you can. Soon it will be too late.

I Cried Today

It's the day before Thanksgiving, 2019, and tomorrow is turkey day.
All is well with me and mine, so why am I feeling this way?

My wife is cooking a feast for tomorrow, and we will all eat our fill.
And give thanks for all our blessings and ask God to keep us in His will.

Yet my heart is heavy, I'm conflicted inside, about some of what I see.
Poverty, corruption, homelessness, and uncaring people around me.

I know I'm older, and age makes one see somethings in a different light.
But singing how you love Jesus and hating others ain't right.

I've got friends and kin in church, people I love and have known for ages,
Who stand by and say nothing as immigrants are mistreated and their children put in cages.

Christian leaders that I've put my confidence in and supported as I thought they did the Lord's work.
Now keep silent about this abuse, lack of healthcare, and the pitiful wages of those that do most of the work.

Maybe I'm judgmental, and I certainly do not intend to be.
But it seems some Christians are reading from a different Bible than me.

I have studied many translations of the Scriptures all my life, and I am yet to find,
The political party Jesus belonged to or that he hung out with the rich folks and bankers of His time.

And remember those "Blessed's" that He pronounced from His Sermon On The Mount?
It was the poor, strangers, children, hurting people, not the rich and powerful He was talking about.

So tears mix with my enjoyment of this Thanksgiving Day.
I cry for the immigrant, the children in cages, the homeless with no place to stay

But saddest of all is the apathy I see in people I have known for many, many years.
Putting politics above all else tends to harden hearts, and I fear we will soon be to the point that no one cares.

Lady Liberty says, "Give me your tired, your poor, your huddled masses yearning to breathe free."
But folks turn away, proving, "There are none so blind as those who care not or refuse to see."

(Prayer: Dear God, may some of the Shoeboxes we packed today find their way to the thousands of immigrant children separated from their families. Please, please, change hearts. Amen)

I CRIED AGAIN TODAY

The Other Side of the Glass

The Coronavirus is still taking lives throughout the land, but folks are beginning to stir around.
On our way to the grocery the other day, we observed a couple of the saddest sights to be found.

We passed a nursing home we often visit where usually one can hardly find a parking place.
Now the lot was nearly empty, and you could park right by the door or in almost any space.

Of course, the threat of the virus has stopped all visitors from coming in.
But we know from experience some older folks never get visits from kin.

We saw several sad faces looking out from the other side of the glass.
Knowing no one was coming to see them, just watching the traffic pass.

How sad it is when our elderly citizens are forgotten and treated this way.
And their children never visiting while only living a few miles away.

During ten years of delivering Meals on Wheels, you would not believe the things I have seen.
Neglect by those that should love their parents, some just spiteful and mean.

With this virus raging, for the economy, some in the government said a few old folks must die.
These are the same ones that say each life is precious. It is, but I can tell you from experience, it's not only babies that cry.

Imagine yourself on the other side of the window. Put yourself in the place of that dear person looking out.
The economy is important, but there are many other pressing needs we should be concerned about.

Life may be treating you well now, you have your health, and riches untold.

But unless the Lord returns or you die prematurely one day, you are going to be old.

The years fly by, the kids move away, before you know it over three-fourths of your life has passed.
So, visit that loved one, talk to the stranger, and don't end up alone on the other side of the glass.

War

I am grateful for our freedom, and the wars fought to keep us free.
But looking back over one hundred years, WW2 is the only war that makes sense to me.

Korea, Vietnam, can you tell me what the US was fighting for?
Or why so many young men lost their lives in those wars?

And look at the Middle East, it's never been stable.
They've been fighting each other since Cain killed Abel.

Now, this is not meant to diminish the sacrifice of those that have died,
Nor the wounded and those that served this country with pride.

They answered the call, leaving family and home, serving, and fighting in a faraway land,
But often wondering what the objective was, in the absence of any real plan.

What causes these wars I often wake up thinking at night,
Religion, politics, gasoline, or is it people that we just don't like?

Old politicians, kings, and dictators, with gigantic egos to satisfy,
Serve as warmongers sending armies of young folks into battle to fight and to die.

One can look at this lunacy and madness in a lot of ways, but here's what I figure,
There would be no more wars if the old men that start them were the ones pulling the trigger.

Fall

What is it about Fall that makes it different from the other seasons of the year?
Oh, I mean apart from what the almanac says, and other clichés that one hears?

I have been blessed to see seventy-five Falls come and go and here's what I find:
More than any of the other three seasons we have, Fall seems to be a state of mind.

It's a feeling you get, a feeling deep inside that you cannot explain.
A sense that one's life, like the turning of the leaves, is beginning to change.

Perhaps it's that first chilly morning as a wisp of wind blows leaves across your lawn,
Or for the first time since early in the Spring, you have to turn the heat on.

The calendar tells you that the holidays are on the way.
And you start the countdown to a soon to be Christmas Day.

School is back in session, and you can no longer speed through the school zone.
And you again realize how quiet the house is, now that all your children are grown.

Football returns and excitement fills the air as fans cheer on and follow their teams.
And you feel the old juices flow, but the games somehow are not as important as they used to seem.

The leaves are colorful and beautiful, but you have to rake and get them out of the way.
And you realize that snow, rain, sleet, and cold weather will soon be the order of the day.

I think Fall is God's way of telling us to slow down, look around, see how things change.
To be thankful but not complacent, always remembering that nothing stays the same.

And should this be our last Fall on this earth, and if we believe in Him,
As sure as Spring brings new life, we will live and bloom again.

Basketball and Golf

Lots of things in life, I don't understand.
How an airplane flies, man's inhumanity to man.

But these simple problems hardly worry me at all,
When I think of the travesty that exists between the participants of golf and basketball.

An eighteen-year-old steps up to the free-throw line,
The crowd stomps, yells, curses at him like they have lost their mind.

The noise is deafening as he bounces the ball,
And then grows silent as through the hoop it falls.

Now, consider the forty-year-old pro golfer as the putt he eyes.
Shh! Quiet! The crowd is told, no loud talking or sighs.

The putt goes in the hole, and the pro lifts his arm to the skies,
While the crowd around him erupts in loud jubilant cries.

The contrast is stunning to me, and I have thought a time or two,
If the scenario was reversed, how the pro golfer would do.

Sounds

As we go through life, from birth into our senior years,
Sounds of laughter, sadness, joy, and music reach our ears.

Like the sound of a football being kicked on a crisp fall day,
Or the giggling laughter you heard as you watched children play.

The roar of a jet plane streaking across the sky,
Or muffled sounds of sweethearts saying goodbye.

Hearing your child cry right after being born,
Or wish the guy behind you would stop honking his horn.

What about the time you said your first curse word,
And all the other vulgar language you have heard.

The soothing, rhythmic sound of rain falling on a roof made of tin,
Knocking on the door of a stranger that welcomed you in.

How loud your heart pounded when you met that special one,
The crack of the bat when you hit that home run.

The sound dad's belt made as it cleared the last loop of his pants,
I can still hear the licks as I started into my dance.

The sounds of getting married, lovers softly saying: "I do."
Sometimes things happen, and those words become "we're through."

"Gentleman, Start Your Engines" means you are at the car races.
"They're Off," says you are watching horses thundering through their paces.

A ringing phone is always something with which you have to contend.
It may be a robocall or a message from a dear friend.

Out in the country where we lived long ago,
It was so quiet in winter; you could hear the falling snow.

Or the sounds of nature, far too many to list,
Wind howling in the pines, birds chirping, a babbling stream, dewdrops from a morning mist.

And what about the many different sounds you and I have heard here today?
Sounds of laughter, joy, and sadness, expressing love for classmates and friends that never fades away.

One by One

I just got a text from the chair lady of our high school class,
Informing me that another member of our Class of 1961 had passed.

Perhaps a word of explanation would be in order here,
To tell you about that Class, and why each death brings a tear.

Harris High School was in Mitchell County, NC, in the small mountain town of Spruce Pine.
So, from the best high school in the Blue Ridge came the Class, numbering one hundred and nine.

We were, and still are, a very close-knit group that loves each other.
When we get together at our Reunions, we are family, like sisters and brothers.

That is why each death in our "Family" to those remaining is such a blow.
The demise of ANY member of the Class of 1961 diminishes the whole.

We are all in our middle to the late seventies now, so we must accept the trend.
Dying is going to be a natural occurrence as all our lives come to an end.

Still, it's not an easy thing to see classmates go away.
And know that death is something that we all must face one day.

So, once again this year, the Harris High Class Of 1961 will gather in September.
We will laugh, reminisce, then pause and shed a tear for those we will always remember.

I love you all.

The Least of These

"In as much as you have done it unto THE LEAST OF THESE, you have done it unto Me."
So, who was He talking about as He taught the disciples how they should live and be?

I think we all know if we read the Bible, put our mind in gear and study His Word,
It was the poor, downtrodden, and outcasts among us whom He wants to be heard.

Probably the easiest way to discern who Jesus was talking about,
Is to read the Gospels and see where He was found hanging out.

Of course, we know He walked everywhere He went, there were no airplanes.
But had there been He would have condemned those buying them and using His name.

You didn't find Him in the palaces, and banks, with religious leaders or any political party at all.
His anger burned, and He overthrew the money changers and others out of the temple as I recall.

He believed those that worked deserved an honest day's pay.
And would condemn those that misuse and cheat employees today.

If He were here, He would be talking to that drunk in the bar down the street.
And telling how God loves and wants to help the junkies, He meets.

The runaway, the prodigal, the prostitute, He does not condemn or judge.
No one has sinned or fallen so far; they are out of the range of His love.

When you think of "the least of these" I'm sure it would be in order,
For Him to visit and cry over children in cages down at the border.

He would visit Shady Rest, Sunset Village, and other "rest homes,"
And comfort the older generation that is forgotten and alone.

And what about the old soldiers, in poor care because of broken promises at the VA.
He would love them, thank them, tell them to trust in Him for a home in Heaven one day.

Little children, He loves and likens them to His Heavenly Home.
So, likewise, He would be there beside those that are abused, beaten, and alone.

These are just a few of "the least of these" and only a small look at what Jesus would do.
We know who they are, the least of these. Now the question is: what are you…and I going to do?

CHAPTER 9

Work Stories, Intriguing People, and Events

I am a friendly person, by nature, and blessed to have had a long working career. In this chapter, you will read about my thirty-seven years employed for American Airlines. Over this time, I met many fascinating folks, as well as celebrities ranging from Muhammad Ali to Marty Stuart. Through conversations, events, and friendships, I discovered everyone has a story. There is dignity in all work, and people on pedestals usually fall.

Ali

At the old airport in the sixties and seventies in Nashville, Tennessee,
Because it was Music City, we saw a lot of famous people and celebrities.

I was working in Cabin service when through the door my friend Sylvester flew,
And said, "Muhammad Ali is sitting by himself down in Gate Two."

So, I stopped what I was doing, and we hurried down the hall,
And there sat Ali, alone in the back-corner wall.

Sylvester, my friend, was anything but shy,
He introduced us; Ali got up and said hi.

As we walked over to meet him, I remember thinking, "What a king-size man!"
Then as we greeted and shook, I could not believe the size of his hands.

We made small talk for a while, and Ali said he was going to LA,
To meet with his lawyers about the government taking his title away.

We did not spend much time with him since we had to work a flight
We didn't talk about his Vietnam war stance or how long it would be until he could fight.

He was very well-spoken, articulate, and interested in everything we said.
And I remember thinking at the time, Ali wasn't anything like I had read.

But the thing I remember most is that as we left, he stood up and said,
I've enjoyed talking to you guys, and it's very nice to meet you, Ed.

That impressed me because when I meet someone for the first time, it's always the same,
Five minutes after shaking hands, I cannot remember their name.

Now opinions vary, I know, about Muhammad Ali.
But I can say unequivocally the time I met him he was very kind to me.

George Adams Jefferson

(This story is true, but it happened several years ago. What follows is to the best of my memory)

It was past midnight in the Washington, DC, airport; I don't remember the year or date.
I had missed my flight to Nashville, getting to the terminal just as it left the gate.

There was a restaurant open next to a lounge,
I ordered a hamburger meal, found a comfortable chair, and exhausted; I sat down.

I was tired, weary, feeling a little sorry for myself, and very alone.
It's just a little delay, I thought, in a couple of hours, I'll be on the red-eye going home.

I was the only one in the lounge as I ate my burger while eyeing the slow-moving clock.
As I was finishing my meal, an elderly black gentleman came in and began to mop.

I asked him how things were going, and he looked at me with a smile,
Fine young man, he said, but it looks like you are going to be here for a while.

He parked his mop and rolling bucket, wiped his brow, came over, and sat down.
Son, he said, if you don't mind me asking, what brings you to our town?

I told him I was employed with American Airlines, that I had spent the day up on Capitol Hill,
Lobbying on behalf of working people, talking to my congressmen about a health care bill.

God bless you, sir, he said, health care would sure be a big help to me.
I've never had any all my life, and next month, I'll turn eighty-three.

Curious, I asked him his name, about the jobs he had, his family, and why he was still working this way.
He answered hard work was all he had ever known and laughingly said, I guess it's just in my DNA.

There is dignity in work, he said, although at my age sometimes it's hard.
I'm not as strong as I used to be, and it doesn't take me long to get tired.

Oh, I've got three grown children that love me, and I could go live with them any day.
But this part-time job gives me something to look forward to since my wife passed away.

George Adams Jefferson was his name; he proudly told me with a smile.
I was born and raised just over the District line in Manassas, Virginia, from here about twenty miles.

That's an interesting name I said, and as we shook hands, I told him mine.
I was named for presidents, he said proudly, born way before my time.

Mr. Jefferson's countenance suddenly changed, and on his face, I saw a tear as it fell.
Sensing my concern for him, he took my hand and said, don't worry, son, all is well.

He then told me part of his story, a story I'd wanted to hear.
I listened intently, and before he finished, I was the one shedding a tear.

I'm the great-grandson of slaves, you know, in Virginia years ago my people were sold,
To a plantation somewhere near Richmond, is the story I've always been told.

The man that owned them treated them well; my grandpa used to say.
But worked them hard until they couldn't work or until they passed away.

Mr. Ed, you asked me when I started working. I guess I was nine or ten.
How much I have been paid is easy. Minimum wage or below, that's as high as it's ever been.

As to the jobs I've done, none have been too hard or too big for me.
Sawmill, grave digger, pouring concrete, cleaning restrooms, and ten years in a factory.

I've always been a hard worker, raised a family, gone to church, never been on the street,
But you tend to get tired working two-three jobs trying to make ends meet.

We talked for a while, shook hands, and he slowly limped away.
I'd better get back to work; he said with a smile if I'm going to get done today.

I watched him walk toward his bucket, trying to gather my thoughts.
In some ways, he's still a slave I reasoned, though now neither sold nor bought.

How can those that have the power to change things let problems exist this way?
The Bible says the laborer is worthy of fair wages, but that's not what those that pay the workers say.

I thought of the CEO's I had known, the many I read about, their greed and all that loot.
Stock options, jet airplanes, multiple houses, girlfriends, trophy wives, and golden parachutes.

Mr. Jefferson, I thought, old and tired, bent and gray, without complaining, you have worked that way.
Backbreaking work down through the ages, earning tips of nickels and dimes and slave labor wages.

People are no longer bought and sold like property in America today,
Thank God that the stain slavery made on our country, while not gone, is fading away.

But poverty, few good-paying jobs, and no healthcare bring on a new set of ills.
Look no further than city ghettos, rural areas, or the Appalachian hills.

My airplane came, I got on board, and as we climbed, I looked down below,
And thought about Virginia, Mr. George Adams Jefferson and his relatives of long, long ago.

God help us I prayed, this country that I love, a place where hope can still grow,
But so much needs to be done for those hurting, so through You may our love show.

Help us do all we can to lift up others that have it tough traveling life's highway,
Thank You for lessons learned, folks we meet, the flight I missed, and please watch over Mr. J.

Jamie—A Lesson in Courage

Since we retired, ten years ago, my wife and I tutored at Mitchell Neilson Elementary School.
We helped first and second graders with their reading, each Monday as a general rule.

It was there I met Jamie, between the Thanksgiving and Christmas break, and he had quite a story to tell.
Seems his grandparents traveled to Florida, brought him and his brother to live with them, their parents being in jail.

Jamie said his mother and dad had been dealing drugs, and the police raided their trailer one day.
Child Services took custody of him and his brother as the parents were led away.

But here sat Jamie, full of life, happy, talking to, and interacting with me.
Starting a new life, he said, happy to be with Grandparents here in Tennessee.

The holiday break came, and I did not think much about Jamie until we came back a week after Christmas Day.
As he came in to read, I could tell something was wrong. It was then he told me his grandpa had passed away.

Good grief, I thought, and tears began to fill my eyes as I bowed my head. Jamie never wavered as he looked at me and said, "I am all right, Mr. Ed."

There was a lump in my throat so big I could hardly speak.
When I finally whispered, "when?" Jamie answered, "Christmas Day last week."

Then Jamie did something I will always remember until the end of time. Sitting up straight, he looked me in the eye and said, don't worry, I'm just fine.

My grandma and God love me; I'm making new friends; it's much better here than where we used to be.
You and Mrs. Biddix love and help me with my reading, so no need for you guys to worry about me.

I couldn't tell you anything else that happened that day,
As I marveled at the courage of this seven-year-old on display.

That was several years ago, and as time moved on, we lost track of Jamie, and by now, he would be nearly grown.
He's a hero of mine, this brave little guy, as much or more so than any man I have ever known.

The Captain in Gucci Boots

It was a piercing cold, snowy, blizzard-like, January night at the airport in Nashville, Tennessee.
The temperature was about thirty degrees, slush on the ramp, very little visibility.

My crew and I were in position, bringing a loaded 727 into the gate with the front landing light blinding Fred, the wand man's eyes.
He crossed his wands for the Captain to stop, the light being so bright Fred could not see, but to our surprise,

The plane kept coming, and I don't know how he did it, but Fred parked him right on the spot.
Mumbling a few choice words, he rubbed his eyes, and even in the cold, you could tell he was hot.

Out of the corner of my eye, the Captain appeared, walking through the mush in his Gucci boots as best he could.
In thirty-seven years, I had dealt with many irate American Airlines Captains, and I thought, this ain't good.

He motioned Fred and me over and asked Fred if he was the one that guided him into the gate.
Yes, I was, he said, and you didn't make it any easier on me with that nose light shining in my face.

We were both shocked when the Captain said I'm sorry, it's the first time I've been here at night.
I didn't realize the nose light was still on as I looked for the line and made my turn to the right.

It's a miserable night he continued, and I really appreciate what you guys and gals do.
And you don't need some Captain making things harder than they already are for you.

With that, he shook our hands, turned in his snow-covered Gucci Boots, and walked away.
Fred and I stood there stunned, shocked at what had just happened, not knowing what to say.

Finally, I said Fred, my man; I wish we had a camera so we could have recorded what just took place.
If we live to be a hundred, we will never see another Captain shake our hand and apologize face to face.

I never saw that Captain again, but if I had, I would have given him a salute.
And remind him of the night in Nashville when he came slushing through the snow in his Gucci boots.

Experiences

In my lifetime, I have seen lots of beauty, devastation, and change.
Good and bad, big and small, and a whole lot I cannot explain.

I cannot explain how it felt to fly in a vintage B-17 bomber from World War Two,
Imagining what the young men that flew it in wartime had to go through.

How can others understand when you tell of Katrina if they were not there,
To see the destruction, loss of life and hope, smell and breathe the toxic air?

How can you explain how you felt when the Towers fell on that fateful September day?
The deaths, the hero's, the tears, the pure horror, and having our sense of security go away?

We are told that death is inevitable, that we begin the process of dying on the first day of our life.
Yet that is of little comfort as you grieve the loss of parents, children, husband, or wife.

But let's not dwell only on unexplainable events that are tragic and bring us to tears.
Look at the beauty we cannot describe that we have seen or been a part of over the years.

For instance, how do you explain to someone that's never been,
How it feels to stand on the Grand Canyon Rim?

The beauty of sunrise and sunsets on Hawaii beaches or an Alaska bay,
Snowfall in the Rockies, the mighty Mississippi River, or the Blue Ridge Mountains on a clear day?

The thrill you get when you watch that first home run clear the fence to win the game.
Yet that feeling is doubled and tripled when your sons and grandson do the same.

The feeling you got when you met the love of your life, the emotion of that first kiss.
The pride when your children were born, the uncertainty of being a parent, and how you would handle this.

The joy of growing old, exploring new horizons, slowing down, not having so much to do.
Relaxing, listening, laughing, helping, loving, sympathizing, advising, and enjoying the view.

What a beautiful world we live in, so enjoy it, and embrace it, explore it as you go along.
The Bible says life is like a vapor. It appears, and in an instant vanishes, and is gone.

So do the best you can in this old world, don't worry, and enjoy the ride.
Change what you can, pray for the rest, and always let God be your guide.

B-17

When I was born in 1943, World War Two had been going for about a year.
Dad was drafted and, after basic, was sent to Europe with the Combat Engineers.

Now I'm an old man, set in my ways, stubborn as I can be.
But World War Two was the last War this country fought that made any sense to me.

I was too young to remember anything that happened at the time,
But as I grew older, studying the War became a passion of mine.

Over the years I've watched films, read books, done all I can,
To educate me and learn about the hero's that defeated Germany and Japan.

I was always fascinated by the air war and the planes flown by brave young men.
Many types of airplanes helped win the War, but my favorite was the heavy bomber, the B-17.

Now I don't believe in reincarnation. We live, we love, we laugh, we cry,
Get married, raise a family, try to help others, then we die.

But if, just if, I lived in some other time, or place, near or far,
I believe I flew one of those big B-17 bombers in the War.

So, on my 70th birthday, you can imagine my surprise,
When my two wonderful sons handed me an envelope that brought tears to my eyes.

Inside was a ticket and a picture of the B-17 bomber I knew so well.
My sons had bought me a flight on a B-17, the Memphis Belle.

I wish I could describe how it felt to fly in the radio man's seat of that grand old plane that day.
But words fail me, and I can't. Some things are so amazing that there is nothing one can say.

I am grateful for Tommy and Bobby that knew my passion and cared enough for old Dad,
To fulfill a lifelong dream, and give me one of the best days and birthdays I have ever had.

The Small Box

As a general rule, the men on my crews that worked airplanes for American Airlines over the years,
Were a brawny, gruff, rugged, sometimes profane group, and very few things gave them pause or fear.

There was one thing, though, that I've seen reduce the strongest and toughest to tears.
Brought a hush to conversation, stop them in their tracks, and some would react as if it was something to fear.

That something was a small rectangular box that would be in the belly once in a while.
In that small box was a coffin, and in that coffin would be the body of a little child.

I've had big callous men say, Ed, will you carry it to the cart for me, some removed their hats as we walked away.
It didn't happen often, but it sure did touch all of us and put a different perspective on the day.

Sometimes grieving parents were waiting at the freight house; other times, the little box just sat there.
One had to wonder what had happened to the little one, and I always uttered a prayer.

We often handled bodies of adults on the flights that we worked each day.
But the body of a child seemed to affect each one in a different way.

I can say, however, that dignity and respect from the toughest of men was always the order of the day,
Anytime we handled a coffin, especially the body of a child on the ramp at BNA.

Marty Robbins

Working at the airport in Nashville, Tennessee, Music City USA,
I would see a movie or country music star nearly every day.

Most were friendly people, talking and signing autographs as they went to or from their flight.
A few did not want to be bothered, telling folks to leave them alone and get out of their sight.

I was laid off from Berry Field Nashville (BNA), working at Dallas Fort Worth (DFW), flying back to Nashville once a week around dawn.
I was dozing alone in the lounge when Marty Robbins sat down beside me and spoke with a yawn,

Hey man, he said with a grin, you look like you've been here all night.
Don't tell me you were that worried about missing your flight!

I laughed, told him no, about being laid off and flying standby.
How I missed the family and wanted to get on the first flight I tried.

He was genuinely interested, and we talked like we were old friends.
As I recall, he asked me more questions than I asked him.

Two ladies came in, and you could tell they recognized Marty, and with camera in hand,
Asked him if they could take his picture, and they were his biggest fans.

Sure, as long as Ed can be in it also, Marty said with a grin,
The woman looked startled and said, "I don't know him."

We both laughed as I got up and out of the way.
The ladies got a picture with Marty Robbins, making their day.

We shook hands with each other, and he said good luck on your way,
And I hope you are soon back with your family in BNA.

I never saw Marty again, and shortly after our encounter, he died.
But I remember him as a real gentleman and think about our visit with pride.

Nice Outfit Ma'am

There are those folks that have a natural flair,
For telling a story and making you feel as though you were there.

Sylvester was his name, and he was a friend I worked with for many years.
He's gone now, but I remember him with both laughter and tears.

A proud black man, a great athlete in his day,
Syl could make a story come alive in his unique way.

Now this story happened at the old Nashville airport many years ago,
In the middle of the day when passenger traffic was slow.

Security was almost nonexistent before everything got so bad.
As I recall only one cop for the whole airport, that was all we had.

So, in this scenario, Sylvester is coming back from lunch, walking alone up the hall,
When he hears the tapping of high heel shoes coming out of the ladies' restroom stall.

As he looked, he saw ankles, knees, breasts, and thighs,
And to hear him tell it, the lady had blue eyes.

In his words, Syl said; here I am, the blackest man you will ever see,
All alone in the hall with a naked white lady.

The thought ran through his mind he said, as he told this story to me,
Ain't none of you white boys around when you need them to be.

So, what did you do? I asked him, did you go in the men's room or turn around?
Nope, Syl said; I just tipped my cap, kept walking, and said "nice outfit Ma'am."

She was a stripper from Printers Alley, and this was a publicity stunt for her act.
Photographers and TV stations were alerted before a limousine took her back.

This was just one of many stories Sylvester described from the beginning to the end.
He's been gone for some time now, and I dearly miss my co-worker and my friend.

Rest in Peace, My Brother.

Jet Fumes

The year was 1966 as I remember,
That my career in aviation began in September.

From DCA to Nashville then to Big D,
Then four years later, back to Tennessee.

Small airplanes and wide bodies, I worked them all,
Loading, unloading, no job too big, no job too small.

Heat, bitter cold, snow, sleet, and rain,
I worked through it all and didn't complain.

Then after thirty-seven years, I suddenly quit.
And now that I'm retired, I don't miss it a bit.

The N-Word and the Country Music Star

I worked with a good friend named William several years back,
We worked for American Airlines in Nashville, and as it happened, William was black.

We had been to lunch in the airport restaurant and were walking back up the hall,
When we met a drunk country music star and his entourage that forced us to the wall.

The so-called "star" was famous, but I will not dignify his name.
His songs topped the charts back then, and he's in The Hall of Fame.

That he had too much to drink was evident for all to see,
Neither will I use the language he directed at my friend and me.

"What's that n—— doing here, get him out of my sight."
"And you, white boy, why are you walking with scum like him, that ain't right."

I stopped, turned toward him, told him to stop his talking,
William grabbed my arm and said, just keep walking.

To hell with "keep walking" I thought as my pace started to slow,
It's not worth it, Ed, my friend spoke, just let it go.

Behind us, the cursing continued, as those with him tried to calm the singer down.
William's expression, on his face, never changed, not even a frown.

When we got to the ready room, I was shaking I was so mad.
I said, Man, how do you put up with that? He looked at me and said,

It's something you get used to; William replied with a sad smile.
It doesn't often happen, just every once in a while.

My temper being what it is, that day, a valuable lesson I learned.
Dignity, respect, and honor are traits that have to be earned.

I knew William was a good man, a man that did what was right.
But the way he handled that situation made me see him in a whole new light.

It's terrible what some have to face, insults, cursing, things that make you want to fight.
But my friend displayed as much courage as I have ever seen in a man that night.

The very best and worst in people I saw on display.
And I weep when I see our leaders fan the flames of racism today.

As I try to make sense of folk's actions, one thought I cannot escape.
Some people are just plain mean, and evidently need someone to hate.

The so-called star soon faded, I think of him now and then.
He's dead now, and I hope he repented, but I never listened to his songs again.

Lake Greeson

Many pleasures God grants us on earth as we go from season to season.
One of the most pleasurable in the fall is to go to Murfreesboro, Ark. and fish Lake Greeson.

Lake Greeson is on the Little Missouri River, filled with all kinds of fish, but mainly striper and bass.
Located miles away from everything, a sportsman's paradise, with all one could ask.

Into this beautiful place, I came for the first time over forty years ago.
With my friends, DP, Doug, and Joe.

We always went in early October, when nature had the mountains and leaves at their peak.
We would stay in a rustic cabin, overlooking the lake, and we would be there for about a week.

The fishing was up and down, and the locals said it was not that great in the fall.
That often aggravated Joe and DP, but it really didn't bother me at all.

While I enjoyed fishing the lake, the beauty, and all there was to see,
What I enjoyed most was the camaraderie and friendship, especially with my best friend DP.

Doug soon quit making the trip, and American Airlines called me back to Tennessee.
But the first week, or so, in October, we would always reconvene, DP, Joe, and me.

I don't remember much about the fish we caught, the weather, or the storms that kept us off the lake.
I do remember the warmth, friendship, tall tales, and never knowing what direction our conversations would take.

We talked mostly about family, our hopes and dreams for our children and grandkids.
And DP and I always agreed we had wonderful, fulfilling marriages, and we're so thankful we did.

In later years as we faced our mortality and the shadows began to grow,
We would sometimes wax nostalgic and wonder which of the three would be the first to go.

We always knew the day would come when in this beautiful place, we would no longer be.
But neither Joe nor I with our health problems thought the first to go would be DP.

I got up this morning, although it's still summer, there was a bit of a chill that said October would soon be here.
The leaves will turn, the fish will jump, Greeson will beckon as it does each year.

But this October will be different from the forty-one that have gone before.
Three old fishermen won't be there; actually, the two that's left probably won't be back anymore.

It was great while it lasted, but all good things come to their end, that's how it must be.
But one day before very long, my friend DP will welcome me to Heaven with a hearty, "Let's go fishing ET."

Fall Fishing Finality

Yesterday Margaret mentioned it soon would be time for the Craft Fair in Bell Buckle, Tennessee.
And I felt a touch of sadness because Craft Fair time always meant fishing time for me.

It's not only the mention of the Craft Fair that causes me to feel so sad.
It's thinking of all the great fishing trips to Lake Greeson I've had.

Three old fishermen, Joe Clark, DP Davis, and me,
Have been faithfully fishing there the second week in October since 1983.

But this year is different; I realize as the leaves began to fall.
Sadly, it dawns on me. There will be no more trips at all.

You see the heart and soul of the trip, and my best friend has passed away.
And I still wake up some mornings thinking, DP will call about our fishing trip today.

And say, ET, I've got the cabin rented, start gathering up your gear,
Can't you see them fish jumping? The time for fishing is almost here!

And I'll tell him not to worry about me, better try to catch a bigger fish and win the bet.
He will laugh and tell me, (and it's true) my friend; you know you have never beat me yet!

Try to get some better food this year, I'll say, maybe some barbecue and steaks, instead of all them beans.
If you don't like what I get big boy, DP will reply, then you do the buying and shopping, by all means

But this conversation won't happen, and I know all good things come to an

end.
But Bell Buckle, October, and falling leaves only tend to remind me how much I miss my friend.

The pain's not as bad as it was for a while, and I handle it the best I can.
I pray every day for his family, his son, daughters, grandchildren, and for his wife, Jan.

And sometime around the second week in October, I will look toward the west with bowed head,
And thank God for thirty-five years of fishing at Lake Greeson, with DP Davis, the best friend I ever had.

REST IN PEACE, MY FRIEND

A TRUE Fish Story

Ahh, I can almost see you there as you read the title and start to turn away.
But the word TRUE kind of grabs you, so you decide to see what another fish liar will say.

Well, what I'm going to tell you I will swear on the Bible is true, if you wish.
'Cause it ain't nothing to be proud of when you are beaten by a fish.

I was fishing at Lake Greeson in Arkansas with my good friends DP and Joe.
We've spent a week fishing there in October for thirty-five years or so.

Now growing up in the mountains, I was very adept at fishing for trout.
But when it came to lake fishing, I was still learning, and both friends helped me out.

Still, I took a lot of kidding since I was a work in progress; there was much I did not know.
Both DP and Joe would tell you that they gave up teaching me anything a long time ago.

One time the boat was moving up into a cove, and nearly asleep, I slowly fed out my line.
When suddenly, the rod and reel were jerked entirely out of my hand,

snagging on the seat, and I grabbed it just in time.

So, the fight was on, him running and the reel humming as through the water he went.
I was up and down with the rod, from one side of the boat to the other, and yelled to DP, "Get the net!!"

Suddenly he stopped running, and I started reeling him in, and about 100 feet away, he came to the top.
Oh my gosh, said DP, what a fish!! Keep reeling and fighting him; give him some slack, but don't stop.

The battle went on for a few more minutes as I reeled him in closer and closer to the boat.
Then suddenly, he came full body out of the water, slung that lure out of his mouth, barely missing my throat.

I sat back down exhausted, and as we all calmed down, I asked my buddies what I did wrong, what did I miss?
They laughed, this time sympathetically, and said nothing, ET. You were just beaten by a fish.

They Come, They Go

On 9/17/66, I began my career with American Airlines (AA) at Washington National Airport, known as DCA.
Little did I know about the twists and turns I would experience in the thirty-seven years until my retirement day.

I crawled up in the belly of a DC 6 that day with George, and I wish I could remember his last name.
A proud black man in his sixties, forty-some years with AA, and the highest seniority was his claim to fame.

Son, he said, I've seen it all in my time, worked with all kinds of people on all types of aircraft.
But one thing I can tell you. Every airplane that came in here eventually left.

I really liked George, was eager to learn, but kind of puzzled at what he was trying to say.
Some leave on time; he continued, some in an hour, a day, sometimes a week. But they all go away.

So, take your time, work safely with your crew, and do the job right.
Because when you finish and push this one out, in comes another flight.

I worked with George, and he mentored me for about three months after I was hired.
A couple of months later, I remember going to a hurried-up party held for him on the day he retired.

I have heeded his words of wisdom for my career with American Airlines and actually throughout my life.
Doing it the correct, safe, way with respect for others and knowing it's a long haul, saves you a lot of grief and strife.

Here's to you, Mr. George. I know that by now, you have gone to your place of rest.
May you Rest in Peace, and thank you, Sir, for a good life lesson that helped me do my very best.

Show Your Badge

After 9/11, as anyone that flies knows, security became tight, on the plane, in the terminal, and on the ramp.
We were to challenge, per the FAA, anyone that didn't have a badge and have them escorted out.

So, with that in mind, we were working a 757 on gate eleven, and the Captain was doing his walk around.
My gate Captain, Fred, saw him, looked him over, and no badge on him could be found.

For this reason, Fred asked to see his badge and a resounding &$&@& you was his reply.
Fred started over to me, but I motioned him back because I had been watching out of the corner of my eye.

I walked over and told the Captain I needed to see his badge. ##%**€ you too was his reply.
I am a Captain for American Airlines in full uniform, so I don't have to comply.

Captain, I said, you will show me your badge, apologize to Fred and me before this day is through.
So, I wasn't really surprised when he got in my face, and out of his mouth came another @%#•¥# you.

I turned to my crew that by now had all gathered around.
And I told them to stop unloading and shut the whole thing down.

Got my supervisor on the radio and laid out the problem we had with a Captain gone wild.
He said to finish the plane, and he would get the Chief Pilot to take care of this spoiled problem child.

We finished the trip. The supervisor called for Fred and me to go inside the gate.
There stood the Chief Pilot and my cussing Captain looking at me with both contrition and hate.

He mumbled something about how words get jumbled up and sometimes don't come out as he would like.
I said, are you apologizing Captain, if you are sorry, just say it. It's easy when you mean it and say it right.

He did, halfway anyway, then he said, is that all you need from me today?
I said, not quite, sir. Show Fred and me your ID badge, and we will get you on your way to LA.

Fire flew from his eyes. His face was crimson red as he fumbled for his ID in a billfold of faded gray.
I looked at it, had him show it to Fred, gave it back, and told him to have a safe flight and a nice day.

Marty Stuart

My former Pastor, WD Thomason, is a dear, beloved friend of mine.
WD retired several years ago, but he still fills in for others from time to time.

He was my Pastor in the seventies at First Baptist Church (FBC) in Smyrna, Tennessee.
It was there we both met Marty Stuart, barely a teenager, but playing on the Grand Ole Opry.

Marty, at that young age, was a talented musician, playing anything with strings.
He toured with Lester Flatt and Earl Scruggs playing venues all over the land, earning his country wings.

Yet when he came home off a road trip or playing the Opry, and he had a day off or two,
Sunday would find him faithfully at FBC in Smyrna, sitting with his mother on the pew.

Marty became a star in country music, but he always considered WD his Pastor and friend.
He called him, over the years, to talk about spiritual matters and advice now and then.

While Margaret and I have met Marty a few times, he would probably not remember her or me.
But I feel like I know Marty Stuart pretty well through my fifty-year friendship with WD.

Marty, and his wife, Connie Smith, a star in her own right, perform genuine Country Music wherever they may be.
They often play to venues with thousands of people and, for years, had a show on RFD-TV.

Marty has taken on the unofficial role of preserving the legacy of Country Music before it is gone.
He is establishing "The Congress of Country Music" in Philadelphia, Mississippi, where he was born.

Marty and Connie share their faith wherever they go, and many times after a long road trip they will be,
Giving a concert at some small church in the Middle Tennessee area for their trusted friend WD.

That's where Margaret and I see Marty, Connie, his band, The Fabulous Superlatives, every time we can,
And marvel at the youngster we knew in Smyrna years ago, his success as a singer, and as a man.

You see, in my thirty-seven years working for American Airlines at the airport in Nashville, Tennessee,
I met plenty of country music stars, and not all are as they appear to be.

Marty and Connie, however, are the real deal, upstanding people, the kind you love to know.
I thank God for them, their faith, their music, and the goodwill they spread wherever they go.

Godspeed and safe travel out on the road.

CHAPTER 10

Friends and Friendships Matter

I have been blessed with a multitude of friends in my seventy-seven years on this earth. In the following pages, you will meet some of them. I consider all of them to be genuine friends, past and present. Friendship is one of God's greatest blessings. Cherish the gift of a loyal friend and be that friend in return.

Old Friends

Age brings on nostalgia, and I feel it in so many ways.
I guess it's natural in the winter of life as we begin to countdown our days.

As 2020 dawns, I look back on a decade gone too fast, especially last year.
And think about the friends I've lost, people that to me were very dear.

But we must not dwell in the past, at least that's what I've always been told.
Yesterday is a past due note. Tomorrow is a promissory note. Today is pure gold.

With that in mind, I will forge ahead into a brand new year.
And thank God for my friends each day they are here.

One thing has always been a problem for me, one I'm still trying to work out,
Is expressing my true feelings to those I really care about.

Not knowing what another year will bring, my friend, this is my message to you.
I won't go into the times we've had, more good than bad, other things we lucked our way through.

Just suffice it to say we have been good friends for a long time, this is true.
And very few people in the world know me better than you.

So, I'll wrap this up my friend, and express what it took me this long to say,
I thank God for you; I love you, pray for you, and your family every day.

God bless you all.

Real People

I have always been a people person, and I try to make friends wherever I go.
Some you feel closer to than others, that's just the human connection, you know.

A basic requirement if you are to be a real friend to me,
Is to be a "Real Person," not arrogant, pretentious, or a phony.

Define "real person," someone asked me one day.
It's a legitimate question, and I answered this way.

A real person does not change, no matter what kind of people they meet.
Minister, banker, movie star, politician, immigrant, minority, those on the street.

A friend that's a real person rejoices with you when you have the world by the tail,
And will pray for you, pick you up, and offer all of their help when you fail.

Will true friends falter and disappoint you now and again?
Of course, they will. No mistakes were made by only One Man.

Real people don't gossip; they pretty much live and let live.
They make up their minds and are quick to forgive.

A real person is loyal, and true no matter what turns life takes.
They will not abandon you for missteps you may make.

It's a sad thing we see with some Christians today, but it is a fact,
Christ forgave them, but on others, they will turn their back.

Somehow feeling superior, talking about others, believing a lie,
Never once thinking, but for the grace of God, go I.

May we try to be "real people" as we travel life's highway,
Showing real love, sharing Jesus, and being a friend to all we meet today.

A True Friend

You know the old country saying
You have heard it again and again,

You have no choice in parents or family,
But you can pick your house, your spouse, and your friends.

Another saying for us all,
We are lucky indeed if we have five true friends, we can call.

What constitutes a true friend, is a question we ask,
Because in our lifetime, people move through so fast.

So, in the next few lines, I will try to write down,
The qualities and traits of true friends I've found.

A friend will visit you when you're in jail,
A true friend will comfort you from the next cell.

A true friend knows of your failures, faults, dreams, and plans,
But always respecting you as his friend and a man.

Should you need a loan sometimes in a crunch,
Payback is never mentioned; the only question is how much?

Time and distance often will separate true friends
The phone rings, one says I need you, the other says when?

True friends in sickness and death don't say a lot of words,
They stand by your side quietly, while others are heard.

As I walk slowly into the sunset years,
I am more thankful than ever for true friends I hold dear.

I've said quite a lot about what a true friend should be,
And I hope you, my friend, will find these traits in me.

DP (Dave) Davis

I came to work at the Dallas Airport in August of 1982; I don't remember the exact date.
It was a few weeks later that I went into Mobile after working the gates.

One day several of us laid off in Nashville were talking about home,
When this tall, lanky fellow behind me said, "just how far back in the hills, are you from?"

DP Davis was his name, he said, as his head turned to me with a grin.
We shook hands, and a lifetime friendship began.

I've lived long enough to know that God works in mysterious ways.
And He gave me one of the best friends I ever had that day.

We worked together, and our families got to know each other,
And now nearly forty years later, I think of Dave more like a brother.

He taught an old mountain boy about fishing on the lakes and how to catch bass.
Let me use his boat and equipment and answered every question I asked.

My only problem with him over the years has been,
In fishing, you never hear the end of it when he wins.

We decided to go back to Nashville when I bid on a Crew Chief job one day.
And Dave and Jan bought our house when we moved away.

Though apart we've kept in touch over the years and each October,
We manage to fish at Lake Greeson in Arkansas, one way or the other.

Margaret and I had our fifty-year anniversary celebration and much to our surprise,
Through the door came Dave and Jan, all the way from Texas, bringing tears to our eyes.

Now time has passed, age and occupation have taken its toll.
It's doctors, operations, hospitals, plus the fact we're just plain old.

But one thing we know for sure is that before long we will be able,
To be where there is no more pain and enjoy each other forever around God's table.

I love you, my friend.

WD Thomason

Friends are some of God's greatest gifts to you and me,
And I feel so honored that one of my best friends, in this life, is WD.

He came to Tennessee from Georgia, many years ago, I heard,
Telling folks how God loved them, preaching His Word

In the early seventies, I first met WD when he became my Pastor,
I was working, raising a family, not thinking much about the hereafter.

Although saved at thirteen in a revival at an old country church,
Had I lived as I should since that night long ago? No, not so much.

WD's gentle spirit, his love of people, and helping those in sickness and strife,
Led me one Sunday morning at age thirty-four to come forward and rededicate my life.

Many years have passed since that extraordinary day.
WD pastored other churches, and my job took me far away.

We met again after he "retired," as God had planned it to be,
On a Wednesday night, at Third Baptist Church Prayer Service, WD, Jackie, Margaret, and me.

That was over ten years ago, and we've enjoyed each other's company plenty.
Have we missed having dinner in restaurants in Murfreesboro? Not very many.

We talk about many things, families, churches, ailments, and sports of all kinds.
But don't say anything terrible about Georgia or Carolina, because that's been our teams for a long time.

Our wives make desserts. We talk, fellowship, and pray.
Thanking God for our time together, for we know all too soon it will go away.

So, on your birthday, my dear friend, may God always keep you in His care.
And may He grant you many more years to serve Him down here.

As I've told people before, of my Salvation, I am as sure as I can be.
Should the Lord return to earth tomorrow, I hope I'm standing next to WD.

Larry Boyd

I can write about sports, cars, growing up, and things that have happened to me without end,
But it's almost impossible to describe my feelings for this dear, dear, closest of friends.

Best, I remember I met Larry Boyd in the eighth grade, in the class taught by Mrs. Young.
And thus, began a beautiful friendship that today, nearly sixty-five years later, is still going strong.

We were together in those days so much of the time,
I would often forget if I were going to his house or mine.

His mom, Susie, was a great cook, and always going out of her way,
To make me feel right at home, and I'm sure Larry felt the same about my mom, Faye.

Sports were a big part of our lives, football, baseball, basketball, and such.
He was a better athlete than me, but just by a little, not very much.

To say we double dated a lot back in the day would be like saying sugar is sweet.
We often took turns driving while the other fooled around in the back seat.

We played football together in high school; I played center, Larry punted and played end.
Our senior year, every time we had to punt, I long snapped the ball to my friend.

We laughed, we loved the girls, we were young and sometimes acted like fools.
Looking back, God was watching over us, or we would have never made it out of high school.

But time moves on, and so did we, leaving those carefree days behind.
Larry went to work for the FBI, I went to college for a year, but marriage was on my mind.

I had married Margaret Willis, my high school sweetheart,
And we wanted to get away from the mountains and find a new place to start.

So, we applied to the FBI, and to our surprise, we were hired right away.
I drove to DC early. Larry showed me around and helped me find us a place to stay.

Before long, my friend's single days were over, and he no longer played the field.
Larry married his true love, also named Margaret, and she was from the West Virginia hills.

I think here might be the place both he and I need to pause and thank our wives.
We married women who made us want to be better men, and truth be told, the two Margaret's probably saved our lives.

Well, we saw the sights, worked and played all night, saw a lot of history in the making.
Young and carefree, getting used to married life, no worries about any risks we were taking.

But as life happens, things are bound to change, and Larry and Margaret moved away.
They were starting a family, and Larry joined the police force in Winston Salem, where they still live today.

They later bought and ran a restaurant as their family continued to grow.
Larry became a pretty good golfer and thought about turning pro.

We stayed in DC for about another year, and then my Margaret was in a family way.
I resigned from the Bureau, and we moved to Nashville, where I went to work for American Airlines (AA).

I worked for AA as a Crew Chief for thirty-seven years in Nashville, Tennessee.
Margaret worked in insurance, as a dental assistant, and office manager as we raised our family.

Thus, began the years of both families earning a living, raising our kids, and we kinda lost touch.
We would occasionally call, exchange Christmas cards, but didn't see each other much.

Time continued to pass, and then one-day lo and behold,
We reconnected and could not believe what we saw: we were old!!

Now we have time to call and talk for an hour or as long as we can.
And I so look forward to when the caller ID shows a call from that "old" man.

We tell the stories of our younger days, and it is true what we infer,
The older we get, have no doubt, the better we know we were.

We get together now as often as we can, once or twice every year or so.
Our hair is gray; our bellies are bigger, and our steps are getting slow.

One thing that does not change is the love we have for each other.
It only grows stronger over the years, and I look at him as a brother.

When we were young, we both agreed we would not live to be feeble men.
But that was before we opened our hearts to Jesus and let the Savior in.

Now I'm excited because in a couple of weeks I will again see my dear friend.
Margaret and Margaret will talk, and we will all reminisce about the olden days once again.

All four of us know we are walking into our sunsets, and thanks to God's Grace we soon will be able,
To eat all we want, have no more pain, and forever enjoy Eternity as we feast around Heaven's table.

I love you, my friend.

Mike Dennison

At seventy-six years of age, I continue to be amazed each day,
At the folks, I meet, and the special friend's God continues to send my way.

I can't remember the month, or year, that Mike and I first met.
But to say the day was Sunday would be a pretty safe bet.

We met in Life Group at Third Baptist Church, Murfreesboro, Tennessee.
Mike could rarely attend because his work was in the area of Washington, DC.

We liked each other the first time we met, and I waited with great anticipation for him to attend.
Little did we know what the future held for both of us as we became good friends.

Prostate cancer would be my nemesis, and a form of leukemia would be what Mike had to bear.
My operation was successful, but my friend had many treatments at Vanderbilt over the next few years.

But God's Grace, the prayers and support of family, friends, and church pulled us through.
I'm cancer-free for five years, and with chemo treatments, a bone marrow transplant Mike will soon be good as new.

My friend is the rare combination of Biblical scholar, common sense,
educated, and a very brilliant man.
He and I have many discussions as we navigate life, family, friends, politics,
and seek God's plan.

One thing I value about my friend is that he has a heart of prayer.
Prayer, to me, is the true mark of a Christian and shows they really care.

Mike and I both realize that God gave us knowledge and a brain,
So, sometimes we think outside the box, instead of the same old thing.

We know that God has cared for us, watched over us, healed us, and shown us what loves all about.
But we keep studying, praying, seeking, questioning, knowing He never frowns on an honest doubt.

May God bless you, Jackie, and family in all your endeavors, my friend.
I wish you health, happiness, and peace until Eternity in Heaven we spend.

Bob Hyland

One of God's greatest blessings in a world filled with hate and strife,
Is when He brings an exceptional person into your life.

Such a person crossed my path several years ago,
From upstate New York, he came all the way from Buffalo.

I first met Bob Hyland on a Disaster Relief trip to Lafayette, Tennessee.
A tornado had roared through, leveling houses and uprooting trees.

We liked each other immediately, and as we worked, we began to feel,
A connection with each other, a brother to brother bond that is real.

Bob is skillful at building most anything, and always willing to lend a helping hand.
Any time I call on him, whatever the task, he is there as planned.

One of the joys for me at Third Baptist Church where we each attend is to see Bob's knowledge grow,
In God's Word, as he studies and spreads the Good News wherever he goes.

Along with his wife, Joann, it is always a wonderful treat,
When Margaret and I go out with our special friends to eat.

It's been my pleasure to sometimes teach the Men's Life Group Class,
And I always appreciate the tough questions Bob asks.

I could go on and on about what this man means to me,
A very faithful friend, confidant, advisor, and someone special he will always be.

As we walk toward our sunset years, our steps are slower, but soon we will be able,
To be where there is no more pain and forever enjoy ourselves around God's table.

I love you, my friend.

Dave Sneed

Many unique people cross our paths in the day to day lives we lead.
One day in 1986, a genuine friend came into my life by the name of Dave Sneed.

Now Dave came to Nashville from Memphis, the City on the Bluff.
Glad to settle down because, like me, he had been laid off enough.

We worked for American Airlines in Fleet Service, loading and unloading the airplanes that came in.
Working in the bag room, mail, airfreight, and cleaning the aircraft cabins.

We soon became good friends, found out a lot of our background, interests, and thoughts were the same.
We both married wonderful ladies; agreed on politics, religion, and too many other things to name.

One thing that bound us together; we were strong Union men.
Both of us had been members of the Transport Workers Union since our employment began.

So, it was only natural when a local was formed that Dave and me,
Were elected officers in Transport Union Local 590.

What followed was a roller coaster ride of nearly twenty years,
Helping members, teaching, meeting, arbitrating, and calming lay-off fears.

Along with another five of the finest men we have ever known,
We kept a young workforce out of trouble and set a peaceful tone.

Still, Dave and I often wish and realize as we take a backward look,
If we had cataloged our experiences, we would have a best-selling book.

But through it all, there in the trenches together, we withstood every attack.
Doing what was right and always watching each other's back.

Now both of our footsteps are slower. Worry and occupation have taken its toll.
Raising kids, operations, and doctor's visits contribute, but face it; we're just plain old.

One thing is sure, as my journey in this life nears its end,
I am so very grateful to have Dave as a loyal, faithful friend.

And one day before long we both will be able,
To be pain-free and forever enjoy each other around God's table.

I love you, my friend.

Norman (Mo) Holt

You know the old saying, you've heard again and again,
You can't pick your family, but thank God; you can pick your friends.

I want to tell you about a real, true friend; I met long ago,
Norman Holt extended his hand to me and said, "Just call me Mo."

Little did I know fifty some odd years ago, on that day, at American Airlines,
We would begin a friendship that would last a lifetime.

We worked airplanes side by side in the sun, wind, snow, and rain.
Whatever was thrown at us, my friend was always the same.

We lived together in an apartment when the air traffic controllers got fired.
We ended up in Texas, where Norman would remain after he retired.

Some folks will find it hard to believe even say it's absurd,
That in all the time we've known each other, we've never had a crossword.

We've shared a lot over the years, our country roots, sports, politics, our faith in God, and what we believe,
Both of us married encouraging women who inspired us to achieve.

Now we live 600 miles apart, and I sure miss seeing my good friend, and he misses me, I'll bet.
Both of us face the problems of health and age as we head toward our sunset.

One thing is clear; soon we will have no more pain and be able,
To eat all we want and enjoy each other forever around God's table.

God bless you my friend and may, in these dark days, you see,
I love you and cannot put into words what you mean to me.

Horace Gaines

I came to work at American Airlines, Nashville, TN, in the fall of nineteen hundred and sixty-seven,
After working in the large airport in Washington DC, the small-scale airport called BNA was like being in Heaven.

It was only a day or two after I arrived; I met Horace. We shook hands, and he welcomed me with a big smile.
Thus, began a friendship that lasted for thirty years until my friend's demise.

We worked airplanes side by side in Dallas and Nashville because of our low seniority,
The hardest jobs and for months on end, the rear bellies of the airplanes would be all we would see.

Horace had a sturdy, athletic build and after playing high school football in his home town,
Went to college and played football in Atlanta, GA, for Morris Brown.

We became very close friends, much like a brother to a brother.
And at different functions, our wives got to know each other.

When layoffs came, Horace and his wife, Martha, preceded us to Fort Worth, TX, where I moved too.
When I got there, they treated me like family, feeding me, showing me things I had to change and do.

After four years, we came back to a built-up Nashville, with flights going to almost everywhere American flew.
Horace worked in Cabin Service; I was a Crew Chief on the line and an officer in our Union, TWU.

Horace proved his friendship again, an excellent sounding board for what was going on.
He never hesitated to give me advice, often telling me when he thought I was wrong.

We had harsh words only one time, in a driving rainstorm, and I don't remember what it was about.
I do know I spent a miserable night, tossing, turning, up and down, my mind full of guilt and doubt.

The next evening my friend met me at the clock. We embraced each other, and the tears in our eyes began.
The "I'm sorries" came from both of us as we promised never to let that happen again.

Horace was a very generous man. Impeccably dressed, creases always in the work clothes he wore every day.
And he loved to tell others what a cheapskate I was, which I definitely am not, by the way.

He loved to get a room full of people and tell them; Ed only carries three dollars in his pocket at a time.
I don't care if he's going to Hawaii, that's all he will have. Here Ed, please take some of mine.

And he would pull out a roll of cash and offer it to me. I'd refuse, and Horace would say, "open your billfold, only three dollars in there, I know."
So, I did, and I always had three ones, just to see him laugh and point, and hear him say, "I told you so."

Horace Gaines passed away much to young and when Jay, Buford, and I went to the funeral home that day,
We were in the room alone with him before the crowd arrived, and we sat silently and prayed.

Horace Gaines was a man's man, an honest, look you in the eye, straight up, faithful friend of mine.
A friend the caliber of which is scarce, he is in my top ten friends of all time.

Rest in Peace, my friend.

My Friend, Ed Hampton, Is Gone

As I came into church this morning, at the very early start to the day,
Steve told me that in the night, my friend, Ed Hampton, had passed away.

I stood there for a moment, a lot of thoughts running through my mind.
This was not unexpected news, but I thought my friend had more time.

I recalled the last time I visited him, how we laughed and talked, and oh the stories that were told.
And he reminded me to get some strawberries for my wife from "just up the road."

I laughingly told him I didn't have any money; I was broke as I could be.
He grinned and said, "that's ok, Ed, you charge all you get to me."

Ed was my friend, but more than that, he was a real person, and that's the highest compliment I can pay.
A real person is the same at all times, honest, a look you in the eye person, not caring what others say.

We became friends later in our lives, and there was several years difference in our age.
But we shared similar backgrounds, knowing hard times, thankful for the way we were raised.

We had a real connection, from the first day our friendship began.
And I am not ashamed to say that I loved that older man.

Ed was a big part of our Sunday School Class, each Sunday, about fifteen of us would study and pray.
On the Sundays I taught, he'd wink and tell me not to be long-winded, that he had other things to do today.

Ed knew cattle, farming, respected the land, and knew the old ways as much as anyone I have ever known.
Sadly, a lot of that knowledge is lost now. As these old-timers pass away, a little more of Americana is gone.

But one thing is sure when I see my friend again time won't matter, and we will always be able,
To talk as long as we want without any fear or pain, and spend Eternity eating and rejoicing around God's table.

And to his family: I go to a lot of homes, I've seen the good and the bad.
Never, have I ever seen a family take such good care of their Dad.

May God bless you. I love you all.

Rest in Peace, my friend.

Norman Ridenhour

I first met Norman Ridenhour at Third Baptist Church in Murfreesboro TN.
We were looking for a new church home, and I went to a class where Norman happened to be.

The teacher, Bob Norris, and the rest of the class seemed just fine.
But as I thought about Norman, the words "smart Alec" came to mind.

And later on, in a Sunday or two, I couldn't believe my eyes,
He seemed to always be joking and hitting on my wife.

But Margaret liked him, and Bob Norris said, "that's just Norman," you know.
So, I began to tolerate him, and little by little on me, he started to grow.

I'm old enough not to make snap judgment till you know what's happened in someone's life.
How they handled the hand they had been dealt, the happiness, the difficulties, and strife.

I found out Norman had more than enough troubles that he owned.
Fortunes made and lost, loss of a child, spent time in the Baptist Children's Home.

Given that, I began to understand where he was coming from; he did things his way.
His attitude is and was you might knock me down, but you'll have to do it every day.

So, a very valuable and special friendship began.
Norman is a Real Person, a trait I bestow on very few men.

By that, I mean he speaks his mind, and you always know where he stands.
Norman really cares for others, always ready to give a helping hand.

We especially enjoyed getting to know his wife, Jackie, as she bravely fought cancer day by day.
We considered it an honor to take her for her treatments sometimes and shed many tears when she passed away.

But Norman, the survivor, carried on, helping in Church, teaching our class.
Playing golf, following his beloved Auburn Tigers, never living in the past.

We now teach our Life-group together, and along with two others, try to stay the Gospel course.
It took four of us, and we still can't fill the shoes of our long-time teacher, the one and only Bob Norris.

We will never agree on politics, and Norman will follow that Party of Privilege, the one-percenters till they either own or destroy the earth.
I, on the other hand, follow the party of the poor and downtrodden, the orphan and the immigrant, trying to get the worker paid what he's worth.

But we agree on what really matters, the Bible, the Gospel, and we both know where we are going when this life ends.
Thanks to what Christ did for us, Heaven is our home, and it sure won't be dull there with Norman, my very good friend.

The Three of Us, Joe, DP, and Me

At Dallas Ft. Worth Airport nearly forty years ago,
I met a toughened old Texan whose first name was Joe.

I was introduced to him by my good friend, David Paul Davis, often called DP,
Who jokingly said I hope after you get to know him, you will still speak to me.

Well, as we were introduced, Joe Clark, said to me with a wave,
You evidently don't care who you are seen with, hanging out with Dave.

I liked Joe immediately and thus began a friendship that has endured all these years.
The three of us worked and fished together, supported each other in good times and through tears.

Folks who didn't know us and heard us kidding each other might,
Think we didn't like each other and were getting ready to fight.

We would laugh and poke fun at each other all day and the night through,
Telling stories, pulling jokes, and kidding as only good friends can do.

For over thirty-five years, the second week in October found us three fishing in Arkansas on Greeson Lake.
We would rent a cabin, bring Joe or DP's boat, and enough food to feed the whole state.

Now I grew up trout fishing in the Mountains of Western NC.
So, this business of lake fishing was pretty new to me.

But my two friends loaned me the gear and took me under their wing.
Taught me all the rudiments of lake fishing and a thousand other things.

The first time we went, I caught the biggest fish (beginner's luck), and on the rest of the trip, they had a frown.
I never won again, but for thirty-five plus years, I never let them live it down.

I have to say, without any reservation, win, lose, or draw,
Joe Clark is, without a doubt, the best fisherman I ever saw.

Now DP would disagree and tell you about all the fish he caught and the prizes he had won.
But it was Joe that caught the biggest and the most, whenever we got done.

DP said Joe was the luckiest man that ever sat in the seat of a boat.
I think Joe beat him so many times it just got his goat.

Everyone knows with three in the boat; the middle seat is where you do not want to be.
But nearly every time we went out, guess who always ended up in the middle seat—-me!

But it worked out fine because when they aged, neither one could hear,
So, I had to be a megaphone, relaying messages to DP in the front and Joe in the rear.

Some of the best times we had were at days end when the fishing was through.
We would sit in the cabin, eating and talking, telling a big tale or two.

DP did the cooking. I cleaned up, and Joe would tell us what we were doing wrong.
One of us would say, "you come on in here and do it, big boy," and we'd turn, and Joe would be gone.

Our fishing trips had been going on since 1983 until the last year or so.
Last time we were there, as I drove back, I wondered who would be the first to go.

I felt a deep sense of foreboding as I got in my car and drove back to Tennessee.
Something told me this was the last time together at Lake Greeson for Joe, DP, and me.

I am not in the best of health, and neither is my friend Joe.
DP seemed healthy as a horse, but little did we know,

That he would develop esophageal cancer, undergo an operation with only a twenty percent chance of pulling through.
But he did by the Grace of God until it moved into his bones, and then he only lived a month or two.

I didn't get to go to DP's funeral; Margaret and I visited Jan and him just a couple of months before he died.
Joe said the funeral was nice, and I'm sure it was, but I sure miss my friend and cannot count the times I've cried.

Somewhere out on Lake Greeson next fall, the fish will be jumping, I know.
But now there are only two fishermen left, and they are too broken down to go.

But guess what Joe, if DP could contact us from Heaven this is what I think he would say,

Hurry up and join me, you all. You won't believe the fishing, and the big one never gets away!

So, let's make sure we put our trust in Jesus, the One that died for all our sins. Open our hearts, love Him, and serve Him each day as we slowly walk to our journey's end.

We will all meet one day in Heaven, on the shores of that Crystal Sea.
And we will fish, laugh, and talk together, Joe, DP, and me.

Mrs. Tandy Cook

We were visiting some friends in Franklin, Tennessee when they took
Us to another part of town where we met Mrs. Tandy Cook.

I worked with her husband, Bill, at American Airlines,
As fine a man and friend as you could ever find.

The Cooks welcomed Margaret, and me and invited us right in,
There we met Tandy, and she became a lifelong friend.

A gracious, Southern Lady, talkative, friendly like few people I have known,
It did not take us long until we felt right at home.

It was close to Christmas, and everywhere we looked,
We saw cakes and pies and found out how Tandy loved to cook.

It's a passion that she loves and continues today,
And nearly all that she bakes, she ends up giving away.

God gives special people talents, and we only have to look,
But few match their last name like He gave Mrs. Tandy Cook.

Bill is gone now. Tandy lost her husband, and I lost a good friend.
But we keep in touch with her, and every now and then,

I will go to see Mrs. Tandy, and we will laugh, and talk at the kitchen table,
Reminisce about the old days and what we would do if we were able.

And before I leave, she will say, "I've got you a surprise."
And then load me down with candy, cakes, and pies.

There are special people God puts in our lives if we will only look.
And we thank Him for one of the most beloved, Mrs. Tandy Cook.

Don Ray Howell

What can you say about a friendship that lasts a lifetime and a day?
The relationship on earth is ended when death takes that friend away?

Such is the case with Don Ray Howell, a friend for as long as I can remember.
I met Don Ray when we started the first grade, fall of 1949, in September.

We went through all the grades together as close as friends can be.
But the high school years and after was when he came to mean so much to me.

We played four years of football together on the Harris High Blue Devil team.
And for such an easy-going guy, on the field, Don Ray could be downright mean.

I played center and he played left guard. I remember one particular game we were in,
When on punting down, they put this large, burly guy over me, and he was ugly as sin.

Now my first duty was to get the ball to the punter, chest high, and on a line.
Then I had to block the heavy, brawny, guy, my head between my legs, looking back at the time.

Don Ray, after the first punt, when I had trouble, growled at me with a frown,
He said, "don't worry, I'll get him." And the next time we punted, big, ugly was in pain, on the ground.

High school was such fun for the two of us, playing sports, often double dating and all.
The music and cars of the day, we were young, carefree, and having a ball.

Those high school days came to an end, and our future was at stake.
So, in the fall of 1961, we both entered Appalachian State.

We roomed and commuted together, alternating driving his car and mine.
Not much time for the fun things, studying now took up our time.

I soon found that coaching and teaching were not the life for me.
I worked for the FBI, then began a career with American Airlines in Nashville, Tennessee.

Don Ray stayed at Appalachian, finishing and getting his degree.
From then until retiring, he taught, coached, and influenced hundreds of young lives in Brevard, NC.

Don and I married Margaret's, and we both would have to say,
We married beautiful ladies in every kind of way.

Over the years, we were busy raising our families, but we always kept in touch.
Phone calls, Christmas cards, an occasional visit, high school reunions, and such.

Then came the call from him that he had colon cancer, the same that claimed his brother and Dad.
Seems that was one of the hazards of dry-cleaning fluid in the business that his father had.

I remember the last Christmas; my friend called me, and how we laughed and talked about "the good ole days."
And how I cried when I hung up the phone, knowing we had come to the parting of our ways.

Don Ray passed away, much too young, and for a long time, I questioned why.
But my faith soon told me that all of us are in the hands of One grander than you or me.

I still think of my friend, and thank God we knew each other for those many years.
And because of Jesus, our Savior, one day before long, we will meet again in the land of no tears.

We will hug each other, reminisce, and forever be able,
To feast and enjoy each other for eternity around God's table.

Be seeing you soon, my friend.

Bob and Jewel Norris

Margaret and I started looking for a new church in late December of 2003.
In early spring of 2004, we joined Third Baptist Church, or as it is known by its members, 3BC.

We felt right at home in the Life Groups we visited the week before,
And lo and behold the next week Bob and Jewel Norris, the teachers, knocked on our door.

We will always remember how they welcomed us and made us feel.
We felt we were where God wanted us, and now we knew the feeling was real.

I remember Bob telling me, now our class believes in helping others as we go.
And sure enough, I found myself helping them stain a deck in a day or so.

I cannot begin to tell you what these two servants of our Lord have meant to us these past fifteen years.
We've learned from their teaching, worked together in missions, and prayed together in times of fears and tears.

They joke about being small in stature and that they must have bent down when God gave out that part.
But to Margaret and me, they stand as giants and show size does not matter when you have a big heart.

In the last few years, some health issues have arisen with Bob that they BOTH had to face.
And, true to form, they both stepped up with prayer, faith, dignity, and grace.

At present, Bob is holding his own, although tests, trials, and biopsies are the order of the day.
Still, when you see him, he seems more concerned about others, smiling, saying tell everyone I'm ok.

The most humbling thing that may happen to me in the future or ever happened to me in the past,
Was when I was asked to be one of the teachers that would teach Bob's Class.

I could never replace him. I don't think anyone feels they could.
I feel humbled and honored to stand where for twenty-five years he stood.

So, to you both, we say, God bless and be with you in these days that may seem dark and gray,
And know you have blessed these two lives and many, many, more that travel life's highway.

WE LOVE YOU BOTH.

My Friend, Bob Norris, Is Gone

It was nearly midnight, March 11, in the year two thousand and twenty.
As I went to bed, my head was spinning. Bad news on TV? Believe me, there was plenty.

A deadly virus was sweeping the nation; tornados had devastated part of Middle Tennessee last Wednesday.
Schools were closed, businesses destroyed, some power had not been restored, and another storm was on the way.

But then came the call that for me was the worst news of the day.
One of my dear friends, a mentor, and teacher, had passed away.

Bob Norris was his name, and I said it over and over in the bed as I lay there.
Thinking of what my friend had gone through and lifting up the family in prayer.

Bob had been fighting that evil cancer, leukemia, for many years.
He's in the Savior's arms now, I thought, as I tried to hold back the tears.

I thought of Bob's small stature, but how he was one of the biggest men I had ever known.
How he welcomed me into the Life Group, he taught for over 25 years and made me feel right at home.

Bob taught us God's Word every Sunday, hardly ever missing a day.
We had fish fry fellowships at his and Jewel's home on Super Bowl Sunday.

He believed in showing others the love of Jesus by putting in action what he said.
Often we would be helping someone in the church or holding a service where the homeless were fed.

After Katrina, Bob went with us to New Orleans to help mud-out homes not far from the Super Dome.
It was tough, hard work, and I worried about him, but he held up his end and then some.

It's been a fierce, exhausting battle, and Bob would not have made it as long as he did without Jewel by his side.
Driving the long trips to Nashville for chemo, fulfilling the "sickness and health" promise she made as a young bride.

Many people will be helped because of the medical trials Bob went through.
One of them has FDA approval, so one day, this drug might help you, me, and others and be of great value.

My friend is gone from this earth to a beautiful land, and today he's with his Savior on Heaven's shore.
And I believe, as Bob often said he would be, he is now over six feet tall, not short anymore.

When I called and asked Bob how he was feeling, in that soft voice, he would answer, "Oh, I'm just fine."
And today he truly is. All pain, uncertainty, worry, and troubles of this life he left behind.

But he also left his dear family, and Bob loved you all with a love that knew no bounds each day.
He often talked of how he hoped each of you had that intimate walk with Jesus as you traveled life's highway.

Bob Norris will not be forgotten, and when years pass and his name comes up now and again,
My thoughts will be that he was my Christian friend, teacher, mentor, and a

giant of a man.

I believe if Bob had a message for us today, it would be: Trust in Jesus so one day you will be able,
To come and see me in my new home, and we will forever feast around the Master's table.

Rest in Peace, my friend. I'll be coming to see you soon.

The Queen

One day several years ago, my wife, Margaret, introduced me to this grand lady and said she was the Queen.
Puzzled, I said the USA doesn't need one, England already has one, so I really don't know what you mean.

My wife gave me that look, as only wives can do, and shook her head.
The Queen of our Chapter of the Red Hat Society did you not listen to what I said??

Well, I met Ms. Mary Hirlston, and we got to know each other and talked for a while that day.
We had an immediate connection, and she made me feel so welcome I just wanted to stay.

Ms. Mary had invited all the husbands of the ladies in her Red Hat group to her home for lunch.
Such a spread Ms. Mary put on; I don't know when I had eaten that much.

Her back yard and covered carport provided the perfect place for entertaining, of which Ms. Mary did quite a bit.
Lots of tables, fans, places to park a lot of cars, room to play games, and plenty of chairs to sit.

And Ms. Mary was the greatest hostess you could have ever known,
Welcoming family, the Red Hats, and church groups into her home.

The party that the kids in the family looked forward to was the Easter Egg Hunt Ms. Mary held each year.

Each egg held a prize or money, and as much as a hundred-dollar bill was known to appear.

The American flag that always flies in the front yard of her home can be seen by all that pass by each day.
But Ms. Mary, in her deep love for our country, has paid a higher price than most of us will ever have to pay.

Her beloved grandson, JD Hirlston, was killed in action, fighting for our country in a land across the sea.
I don't know if there are Gold Stars for grandmothers, but in Ms. Mary's case, there ought to be.

She has kept JD's memory alive and honors his life in many ways.
Pictures in her home, supporting our Veterans, and placing flags on graves.

Ms. Mary is getting a little older now than when she recruited my wife into the Red Hats many years ago.
Vision is not what it used to be, she struggles to hear, uses a walker, and her steps are getting slow.

But her faith in God is stronger than ever, and that indomitable spirit keeps her on the go.
She is happier, enjoys life to the fullest, and spreads more goodwill and cheer than anyone I know.

So, here's to you, Ms. Mary, may God bless you every day, and in all that you do.
And if I had to share the woman, I love with someone else; I'm glad it was with the Red Hats and YOU!!

We love you.

One Day

Two men from very different parts of the USA met at the DFW airport one day,
One from Spruce Pine, North Carolina, the other from Gridley, California, three thousand miles away

One had joined American Airlines after serving four years in the Army, most of the time in Germany.
The other signed on with American after four years with the FBI in Washington, DC.

One day DP said to ET, just how far back in those hills did you come from?
ET said to DP, far enough to know I liked it better than here, and an instant friendship was born.

That happened one day over forty years ago,
The ET is me, Ed, the DP is Dave, my friend, just so you know.

Over the next four years, we worked side by side and got to know each other.
Our interests were much the same, and our friendship grew, we saw ourselves more like brothers.

One day a tradition was born when Dave invited me to go fishing in October, in Arkansas, at Lake Greeson,
Which continued for the next thirty-some years. If one of us missed, you better have a good reason.

Now, for me, this required some training, and DP was glad to help out.
You see, being from the mountains, lake fishing was new, I had only fly fished for trout.

Along with friends Joe Clark and sometimes Doug Moore,
Year after year, we went to Murfreesboro, Arkansas, and fished Lake Greeson's shores.

We often talked after a long day of fishing on that lake that we loved so,
How we enjoyed this time together, and as we got older, talked about who would be the first to go.

With DP and myself, a lot of our conversation was about our families, those that we held dear.
And we delighted in telling each other of the family additions and changes when we got together each year.

Margaret and I visited with Dave and Jan in Texas. They visited with us in

Tennessee when they could.
Each time we got together was special, but the annual trip to Lake Greeson was always excellent.

One day I got the call. My dear friend, after getting past one serious illness, was now facing another.
As we talked, I could hear it in his voice. This was alarming, and I knew I would soon lose my brother.

We said our goodbyes to each other that day, tearfully over the phone.
Over the next few weeks, Dave, was constantly on my mind, as he battled the unknown.

Jan kept us informed by text, Margaret and I prayed, so did a lot of prayer partners we knew.
Praying for my friend, Jan, and the family, that God would heal him if He saw fit to do so.

Then one day, the dreaded text came. Dave passed away peacefully, surrounded by the entire family, wrote Jan.
I read the text, and the tears flowed freely as my wife Margaret held my hand.

One day I lost one of the best friends I had or ever will have by far.
But then you cannot really lose someone if you know where they are.

My friend is in Heaven, enjoying all that is in that beautiful place.
Laughing, fishing, helping others, seeing family, friends, and Jesus face to face.

One day, and here's the profound part - One day soon, very soon, thanks to our Savior's love,
I will join Dave, and we will laugh, fish, feast, and forever enjoy our friendship in Heaven above.

One day, someday.

I love you and miss you, my friend.

CHAPTER 11

A Little of This, A Bit of That

Well, I had to have a chapter for some of my writings that didn't quite fit in the other categories, right? Here you will find a bit of humor, sentiment, and just maybe a few life lessons that will lift you up on this journey we call life.

Age

Age is a number. Life is a game.
They exist together, but they are never the same.

They do have something in common though, sort of like a die that is cast,
While they are on the road together, can we agree they both move too fast?

Names

A friend of mine will whine and complain,
If you don't address him by his proper given name.

It's his thing, and it upsets him tremendously I guess,
But for me, it's too insignificant ever to address.

Let me tell you why bungling my name never makes me upset.
It's because I've probably got more names than most people you've met.

My mother named me Edwin Tommy Biddix. I guess she thought it was hip.
Daddy didn't think much of it and said: "we'll call him Skip."

To my kinfolk in the mountains, I was Skipper and Skip from the day of my birth,
But that's just the start of names others have given me on this earth.

I've been called Edwin, Edward, Eduardo, Edgar, Eddie, and Ed,
Tom, Tommy, Thomas, and ET from the movie, so someone said.

I saw the movie at the theater one day, all alone.
And found out why everyone was saying "ET phone home."

If I had a dollar for every time, someone yelled that at me,
I could have retired much earlier, completely debt-free.

Add all this together, and there's almost too much to comprehend.
I answered to each name because in the end,

When it comes to names, I've been called a bunch.
I answer to them all, especially if it's a call to breakfast, supper, or lunch.

New and Improved!!??

Because I'm the one that's writing this, I do from time to time,
Write about something that ticks me off or a pet peeve of mine.

So, it is with commercials that we have to endure for things we buy at the store,
Everything from cars to insurance to butter to drugs and a whole lot more.

But to me the thing that gets me mad, and really tears up my mind,
Is when it says "new and improved" on a product I use all the time.

Take peanut butter, for example. The kind I buy and the only brand I care about.
I look on the shelf where it usually is but, it's hard to find. I guess the store is out.

Then I see it in a brand-new jar. New and improved the flashy multicolored label said.
Upon further inspection, the jar contained four ounces less and cost a quarter more than I usually paid.

That's their definition of new and improved? But I bought it anyway.
It aggravates me, but I love Jif Peanut Butter. What more can I say?

The Forgotten

He worked in the coal mines for nearly forty years, starting when he was 16 years young.
Now he lies in his bed, barely breathing, dying slowly with black lung.

For years he had health insurance, at least that's what he was told.
But no one notified him that the plan had been terminated when the company was sold.

She married her high school sweetheart; in three years, they had three little ones.
Now she works three minimum wage jobs, her no-account husband long ago, leaving her alone.

A month ago, she was overjoyed as the minimum wage was enacted, and she saw a rise in her pay.
Then the places she worked cut her hours, and now she actually makes less each day.

He served his country long, and he served it well. Two Purple Hearts and medals show he paid the cost.
Homeless now, he lives on the street, panhandling, begging, suffering, all his dignity lost.

He's been in rehab hospitals, was getting proper treatment at the VA.
But he relapsed and this time due to lack of funding, they turned him away.

She never knew her mother, who died from an overdose a month before her first birthday.
Now, at seventeen, after living with five foster families, she is running away.

Molested for the past year, as she walks into an unknown future, tears fill her eyes.
And she wonders why those who fought for her birth seem to care so little when she cries.

Two seniors, married nearly sixty-five years, sit holding hands. He can't walk, she has the beginnings of Alzheimer's the doctors say.
Two children live in other states. Health insurance cancelled; they cannot afford the high price of drugs; they have bills they cannot pay.

They smile and kiss, and he turns on the ignition, the garage door is down.
The car is running, smiles still on their faces the next morning when they are found.

This is the America we live in today. Our neighbors, our friends, strangers we see wherever we go.
Are we like the Priest and Levite in the Good Samaritan parable that passes by, pretending it's not so??

I'm sick and tired of hearing so-called Christians say it's THEIR fault, they made their bed, in it let them lie.
Never thinking except for the Grace of God, a twist or turn here and there, it could be you and I.

What's wrong with spending our tax money on our citizens in need?
Better than sending it overseas where some dictator will use it to commit foul deeds.

And don't tell me our leaders and government could not help alleviate the pain and suffering in our land.
We help other countries, spend billions in unnecessary wars, and travels to coddle dictators in foreign lands.

And to those that sing "Oh How I Love Jesus" yet hate the immigrant or those of a different color:
May I remind you that Jesus welcomes ALL people to Him. That means you, me, ALL people with the command to love each other.

Real Men Cry

I've written several times about us macho men, our feelings and such;
How we have to be strong no matter what, showing no emotion, or at least not much.

Well, I have to wonder about the woman or the man,
That doesn't shed a tear or two at some of the things happening in our land.

Oh, I don't mean you have to bawl, and squall, and attention try to seek.
But I have to wonder about you if occasionally a tear doesn't roll down your cheek.

Not all tears are tears of sorrow or pity; there are tears of laughter and joy.
Tears of accomplishment, victory, confession, thankfulness, the birth of a girl or a boy.

I shed a tear at my conversion at Grassy Creek Baptist Church.
And I still do in times of prayer because I know God loves me so much.

A tear of gratitude will sometimes fall when I think of my wife.
I am thankful for her because she, too, helped save my life.

When my two sons and grandson were born, tears of joy, I had to wipe away.
And I worried and prayed I could be the man to lead them to where they are today.

Injustice in this world can, and should make us cry.
To see others mistreated should push us to ask why?

Why the mistreatment of old people and putting little children in cages?
Discrimination, racism, exploitation of the poor, and substandard wages?

Did you cry when the Twin Towers fell, and our security was taken away?
Do you cry for the school, church, and other mass shootings in our country each day?

Do you cry for the soldiers, past and present, and how they have been neglected?
And direct your anger toward the politicians whose only thought is how they can be re-elected?

I could go on and on, but you know your dreams, thoughts, hopes, weaknesses, and fears.
Don't give up. Keep fighting, be thankful, and don't be ashamed to shed a few tears.

My Change, Please

Shopping the other day, something I do not like to do, found me getting very tired.
I had made several stops and, my pockets were weighed down with change I had acquired.

So, on my last stop, I made a purchase of two dollars and fifty cents at a convenience store,
And waited in line to pay the young man at the register who seemed methodical and bored.

Not wanting any more change, I handed him fifty cents and a five.
Which confused the young man as he suddenly came halfway alive.

It's only two fifty he said with a confused look on his face.
I just shrugged, shuffled my feet, and stood in place.

No one was behind me, so I knew I had plenty of time,
I stood there as the young man tried to figure this out in his mind.

He looked at me, then at the computer, then at the fifty cents
Then handing me back the two quarters he said, sir, I don't need this.

Yes, you do, I told him. You see, I don't want any coins back in change today.
He looked back at the register, and for a moment I thought he was going to run away.

I let him stay confused a little longer and then decided I had enough fun.
Son, I said, just put the money in the register and give me back three ones.

Well, it was like the skies parted, and the angel of knowledge descended on his head.
The dazed and confused look left as he finally grasped the meaning of what I had said.

I thanked him as I left, told him I hoped he had a nice day.
Still, I was overcome by a bit of sadness, as I went on my way

What's happened to the education of our young folks in the automation and the instant information age?
Seems it's all computers, tablets, iPhones, and they no longer teach common sense off the written page.

Oh, I know I'm old fashioned, and the old ways of teaching have long ago been put on the shelf.
But, God forbid, one day the grid goes down, and this computer generation has to think for themselves.

Cross Out the Cat

I am, as a rule, not a superstitious person. I don't hold to "step on a crack, break your mother's back."
But there is one thing I do that I have to do, been doing for so long I've lost track.

I guess I picked it up from my dad. He had several superstitions he adhered to since a boy working in the fields.
What is it, you ask? Very simple. When a cat crosses the road in front of you, you X it out on the windshield.

My wife thinks this is hilarious and says, do you think the only cats that cross that road are the ones that you see??
Don't know, don't care, I tell her. Not concerned in the least. It's only the ones in my line of sight that earn a cross out from me.

Black cats are especially heinous. They send shivers up and down my spine. Sometimes I cross them out if they only start across, if they go, then maybe two times.

Got the car washed the other day. The boy saw the faded X's and asked if that's how many times I've been kissed.
I didn't answer the little smart, smirking, nosy, kid. Sure do hope that there have not been any other cats that I've missed.

Hoeing Corn

Some chores I really hated growing up on a farm.
And right at the very top was hoeing corn.

Now I didn't mind fertilizing or plowing the row,
Watering or whatever it took to help it grow.

But to pick up that chopping hoe and beat at the dirt,
Seemed useless to me, and it was backbreaking work.

Now dirt is dirt, I've believed that since I was born,
But Daddy wanted "fresh" dirt pulled up around the corn.

So, I did as I was told, but in my mind, I knew that one day,
There would be a time when I would move away.

And when that time came, and I had to go,
Unless misfortune struck me, I would never pick up another hoe.

Well, I did move away, and we raised a family of our own.
We have never farmed again, but a few gardens we have grown.

I've always helped my wife with the flowers she likes to grow.
Whatever she needs, I'll do as long as it doesn't involve that hoe.

Junk, Memories, and Treasures

If you are like me, every now and then, the stuff I have accumulated starts pushing me out the door.
I'm going to clean it out, throw it away, I say. This ain't going to happen to me anymore.

Boxes for Goodwill, trash bags for the throwaways, trunks, and shelves for what I'm going to keep.
The task will be daunting; I'm going to be here quite a while before it's clean enough to sweep.

Plunging right in, I find some tin cans, why I kept them I don't know.
Some plastic jugs, old moldy rugs, into the trash bags they go.

Some clothes in boxes, old shoes, a clock that doesn't work, kid's books ranging from fire trucks to Jack and Jill.
All these items and several more things that clutter the floor I throw in the boxes for Goodwill.

Getting somewhere now, I think, as I take a break and look at what I still have to do.
Most of the stuff that is left is mine, so before you know it, I will be through.

Plunging right in, I fully intend to clean this place out. No longer will it be a pigsty.
But suddenly, after I move a big old chest, something over in the corner catches my eye.

My goodness! It's boxes of stuff from high school and college, things I had forgotten about.
No problem, I thought, it's just old stuff. I'll go through it and throw most of it out.

Here are the four annuals from high school, chronicling all our high school days.
My first baseman's glove, my football jersey, and a football. Can't throw those away.

A pair of white (?) shoes, a strange-looking comb, a hardened jar of flattop wax and gel.
My football letter, a copy of the Junior play, and several love letters. Better keep those as well.

Old report cards, pictures galore, several pieces of strange clothing and hats.
A 40-yard marker from a football field. Now, where and how on earth did I get that??

Then I discovered another huge box so heavy it was absurd.
Tons of records, forty-fives, and albums, thirty-three and a third.

Elvis, Dion and the Belmonts, The Platters, The Coasters, and Bobby Dee, Marty Robbins, Buddy Holly, Patsy Cline, The Statler Brothers, and Brenda Lee.

Found a box with some memories from college, pictures of parties I had forgotten about.
Some articles of women's clothing (?), a summons to court, better throw those things out.

Sorting went on for hours. Deep in the fifties and sixties, I completely forgot the time of day.
When I finally came back from the past and surveyed the scene, very little had I thrown away.

Then my wife came in, looked at the space I had created, decided that it was just enough.
When she returned to the room, again and again, she was carrying load after load of her stuff.

So, I gave up. It's a battle that cannot be won. With limited space, we still buy more of the stuff we think is nifty.
A little bit of advice here, though. If you are going to clean out your treasures, don't get lost in the fifties.

Crosscut Saw

I was at a yard sale the other day, not looking for anything particular at all.
When out of the corner of my eye, I spied it, a rusty old crosscut saw.

I'll make you a real deal, the farmer said, as he ambled over to me.
I told him no thanks. I'd seen all of the saws I ever wanted to see.

He eyed me up and down and said, how much do you know about saws, cutting wood, and such?
I said, sir, if the saw strokes I've sawed were laid end to end they would reach around the world, that's how much.

You see, when I grew up, three wood-burning stoves meant we had to get wood again and again.
Most of the time, we cut wood when it was too bad to do anything else, like when it snowed or rained.

My Grandpa lived with us, and he always had a wood heater in his room to keep him warm.
A wood cookstove, a wood-burning heater in the living room, requires a lot of trees to be cut on the farm.

My older first cousin, Bobby Lowery, lived near us, not far away.
And many times, he and I would saw and chop trees all day.

Bobby and I loved Grandpa, and it was well understood,
That Grandpa would not ever, ever, be without wood.

But the times have changed, both my cousin and Grandpa have passed away.
I've got central heat and air, and I have not cut wood in many, many days.

So, you see, sir, I know a thing or two about the crosscut saw, how it made my muscles sore.
But no thanks, you keep it or sell to someone else. It just doesn't fit my hands anymore.

Easy to Say, Hard to Do

Love thy neighbor. It shouldn't be very hard,
Until his pit bull jumps the fence and tears up your yard.

What about the old saying, "forgive-and-forget?"
Not quite got the forgetting part down yet?

You love her. She knows that, yet it was you that was wrong.
You need to ask her forgiveness, but what takes you so long?

You stand by the graveside with a friend that just buried a child.
Words won't come. Don't worry, but stay there for a while

He betrayed you, and you haven't spoken in years. Now he is dying, and still, you won't budge.
Go to him and make it right. The heaviest load you will ever carry is a grudge.

If you feel the urge to help someone, then that's what you should do.
If they misuse that help, then that's on them, not you.

Resist the urge to criticize the poor and homeless; their stories will make you cry.
A wrong turn, a bad break, and except for the Grace of God, it very well could be you or I.

Loaning money to a relative? I hope yours are better at repaying than mine.
I've found, though it's painful, a gift with nothing in return will be better sometimes.

Insurance problem, hospital bill, cable company, any other disputed bill to pay??
Gather all your patience, get ready to talk to an automated machine, smile, and don't let it ruin your day.

Celebrate little children even when they are loud and run around bugging you with their toys.
Let them enjoy this fleeting time when all things are new. Let them be little girls and boys.

Respect older people. Oh, I know we are slow and tend to get in your way.
Just take a breath and remember you will walk in those same steps one day.

Well, I could go on and on about what we should and should not do.
But the easiest way to navigate each day is to let God guide you through.

Class Reunion of 1961

We've come from many places to be together today,
The steps are a little slower, the hair either missing or gray.

We talked, laughed, yes, and sometimes even cried,
Reliving old days, telling old stories, remembering those that have died.

We've traveled different pathways since graduation day,
But God's Grace, family, and friends have always shown us the way.

Now we must face the fact, and sunset is drawing near.
We can only look around and wonder, will I be back next year?

And when that curtain falls on me, I want it understood,
That our friendship is one of God's greatest blessings in life, and we were friends, and it was good.

Battlefield

In Murfreesboro, Tennessee, in late December of eighteen hundred and sixty-two battle lines were drawn.
The Battle of Stones River, in the war between the North and South, was set to begin at dawn.

The Civil War it was called, and I've always disliked that name.
There was nothing civil about it. Brother against brother, a terrible, terrible shame.

The battle started on December thirty-one, eighteen hundred sixty-two.
It lasted two more bloody days into the new year before they got through.

The carnage was high on both sides, thousands wounded, captured, or dead.
The locals that helped dig graves and care for the wounded said the Stones River ran red.

I try to go to the battlefield in late December, as the new year approaches and the old year ends.
I stroll slowly among the thousands of graves, trying to imagine how it would have been.

My emotions sometimes get the best of me, and occasionally I will cry,
As I contemplate what happened on that sacred ground, I have to wonder why.

Why, why, dear God, do we humans fight and war with each other and let hate still grow today?
Lord, help us to care and love those different from us and allow Your love to lead the way.

CHAPTER 12

The Circle of Life

In the first eleven chapters, I hope you have enjoyed the journey that has been my life. My wish is that you, dear reader, have been able to identify with a poem that has brought back a memory, made you smile, or strengthened your faith. My family is very important to me. In this final chapter, I have sought to portray where we are today as we look toward the future. God bless you and your family, and may you treasure each moment you have with them.

A Legacy??

How do I want to be remembered when I die? I really haven't given it much thought.
I guess, as someone that did not compromise his principles, one who could not be bought.

I've tried to be forgiving and not give hatred, prejudice, or racism any place in my heart.
I care for and help "the least of these" in whatever way I can do my part.

Remember me as someone who loved old folks and little children and could not stand to see them abused.
One who believed that every person is valuable, no matter how broken and misused.

As someone who loved and sought to follow Jesus, tried hard but so often failed.
And realized the only reason I will ever get to Heaven is that the Grace of God prevailed.

You can say I accepted Jesus as my Savior when I was in my early teens.
Though I drifted many times from Him, He never abandoned me.

Say, I was a Union man and took it literally when the Bible said, "The worker is worthy of what he should be paid."
That I fought for the working people, higher pay, better working conditions, and benefits not to be delayed.

I was honest, paid my debts, and worked hard all my life.
Loved God, country, and family; I was always faithful to my wife.

I was blessed to grow up in a small town, and I am thankful for all my friends. God has blessed me in so many ways, and I have no regrets when this journey ends.

A legacy? Oh, I don't know. My life has been wonderful every day that I've been spared.
I hope folks would remember me with just these two simple words: He cared.

I Must Be Getting Old

My old golfing buddy called and said, hey, want to play a round or two?
I said no, I just got up, got to go to the bank, and I've really got too much to do.
(I must be getting old)

The phone rings, a guy I know says he's got two Titans tickets if I want to go.
It's tempting, but the widescreen and my recliner call me, so I tell him no.
(I must be getting old)

My favorite college team, the Carolina Tar Heels are playing on Channel Three.
But I can't pull myself away from this remodeling program that's on HGTV.
(I am definitely getting old)

Daytona 500, Another racing year is here. Why do I not care anymore?
Because the corporations now rule, and besides, they let foreign cars in the door.
(I'm mad, not an old thing)

A picnic you say, a long walk out in nature, see the birds, eat beside a babbling brook?
Nah, don't think so. I believe I'll sit here in the sunroom and read this book.
(Yep, getting old)

It's Valentine's Day, she brushes by and says, hey big boy, you gonna watch TV or go to bed?
Oh, my goodness! Did I hear that right? Better hurry. I may be old, but I ain't dead.
(Not that old. . . yet)

Wayward Sons

I guess in the life of anyone attempting to raise teenage sons,
Comes a time when you think all your teaching is coming undone.

This happened to us as our two sons went through those teenage years.
Running with the wrong crowd, doing a lot of the wrong things we feared.

Being a man, I somewhat understood more than my wife,
Some of the things teenage boys were going to do at that stage of life.

Still, as a father, you want your sons to act the way they should and employ,
The good judgment, respect, and follow the faith they have been taught as a boy.

A verse in the Bible helped me as we navigated these troublesome times quite a bit.
"Train up a child in the way he should go, and when he is old, he will not depart from it."

I changed one word though, to give us hope for the times we were in:
Instead of "depart from it," I said, "return to it" again.

We got through those years because God in His mercy and love,
"Brought back" two wonderful sons that we are so proud of.

The Operating Room

The diagnosis is in; the insurance has been approved. I will have an operation soon.
A few things I must do, take some new medication, then it's off next week to the operating room.

During the week, lots of friends called and said they are praying for me.
Some folks dropped by, wished me luck, prayed, and said what will be, will be.

This morning my wife and family, my Pastor and a few church class friends,
Met me at the hospital, prayed for me, and stayed with me until the nurse wheeled me in.

There in the prep area, several people hooked me up to all kinds of machines as the clock on the wall said five until noon.
Twelve today, the time I had been dreading as we began the long roll down the hall to the operating room.

Lord, I prayed as we rolled along, here we are together, just You and me, alone once more.
My family, friends, Pastor, and church family are waiting anxiously on the other side of the door.

And I'm scared Lord, even though I've been in this situation before,
So, I ask you, please, dear Savior, go with me through the operating room door.

I have no right to ask you this because of the many times I've failed and had to start anew.
Truth is, and You know this God, I ain't no grand bargain in the Kingdom for You.

Then a Soft Voice whispered to me, My Child, I'm a God of mercy, not gloom and doom.
And I don't know how to explain it, but suddenly His Presence filled the operating room.

That cold table became warm, and all anxiety left my mind, and as the anesthesiologist holding the mask said "goodbye,"
My last thought was if this is my goodbye, then it's all right because I will soon be with Jesus somewhere up there in the sky.

Well, I'm still here, and take it from someone that's felt the operating room chill,
That steel door into the operating room can't keep Jesus out, never has, never will.

Inspired by Christy

The Lady from Latvia

Liene is her name, and she came to America from Latvia several years ago as a teenage girl.
A good tennis player, she came to America on a tennis scholarship and entered a brand-new world.

She played tennis and got her degree at Western Kentucky in the Bluegrass State.
Then came to get her Masters here at MTSU in Murfreesboro after her graduation date.

Liene and our son, Tommy, met, had an instant attraction and true love they found.
This proves once again when it comes to matters of the heart; love knows no distance, country, or bounds.

They had a spring wedding with Liene's parents coming from Latvia to attend.
Held at the Oaklands Mansion, it was a happy gathering of family and friends.

So, that day in late May was an extraordinary one,
As we welcomed into our family, Liene and Jaden, her son.

We were especially proud to go to Nashville and see,
Liene sworn in as she became a citizen of our Country.

We are thankful that God sent Liene and Jaden our way.
They are an essential part of our family, and we love them more each day.

Fall Chills (and Hope)

It's the last day of August in the year of our Lord 2019.
The temperature is in the eighties, and the grass is still green.

But as I look out and see shadows of the trees lengthen against the house wall,
Wind blowing leaves across the lawn, and in my mind, I know, soon it will be fall.

The seasons of the year, so much like the phases of our lives as they unfold.
We are born in the spring, grow in the summer, fall, finds us fading, and in the winter, we are old.

I am now in the winter of my seventy-sixth year, and if truth be told,
Never, ever, in my younger days did I think I would live to be this old.

Yet, here I am, and it leaves me to wonder why,
Why am I still alive when I've seen so many good friends die?

As another winter approaches, the trees will lose their leaves, plants, and grass will be dying or dead.
And as I contemplate the future, I know I have more sunsets behind me than I have sunsets ahead.

One of the many things God blesses us with as time lets us come this far,
Are the wisdom and knowledge to see our lives, our hopes, and dreams as they really are.

I can't speak to anyone else's life. I can only comment on mine.
And try to understand some of the things that have brought me to this particular time.

Born in the mountains of Western North Carolina in March of 1943,
To sturdy, stern, country parents that nurtured and truly loved me.

Made to attend church and school, taught the value of work at an early age,
It was a tough life at times, but I cannot put a value on the way I was raised.

Then came the event in my life that I will always consider the most critical part.
At age thirteen, in a revival at Grassy Creek Baptist Church, I received Jesus into my heart.

Now, if I'm honest, and God knows I want to and try to be,
I've strayed from Him many times since that day, but He has never left me.

The second-best thing that has happened in my life,
Was when Margaret Willis, my high school sweetheart, became my wife.

Jesus Christ saved me; there is no doubt this is true.
But in a much different way, Margaret saved me too

She is my lover, my supporter, my defender, my best friend that calms my fears.
An inspiration to all who meet her, loves God and family, and on Sept. 8, we will be married fifty-seven years.

Sons Tommy, Bobby, and Grandson Aaron are now a big part of our lives in so many ways.
Christians, good family men, and solid citizens, they love us and brighten our older days.

So, here I stand, as shadows lengthen and the wintertime of my life draws near.
And I can't help but wonder, come spring, will I still be here?

I hope so. For there are a few things I still want to see.
Aaron graduate college, a great-grandchild, or two, or three.

But what if spring finds me gone from this life, done, over, through?
Hey, that's no problem. I've had a great life, so that's OK too!

To whoever reads this, I only have a couple of things left to say:
I love you, and I hope you live your life so we can be together again one day.

And sing that old hymn, "to God be the glory, great things He has done,
So loved He the world that he gave us His Son. . .

The Elevator

I don't remember exactly when it was, as I get older, I lose track,
Of how many times I've been to the doctor for shots in my hip and back.

After having both knees and shoulders replaced my back started to give way,
And so, it was I waited for the elevator after Dr. McKissick had given me another epidural one day.

Standing there in pain, I was feeling sorry for myself and wondering why this should be.
Having a real pity party, I felt enough terrible stuff, and operations had already happened to me.

As the elevator door opened, with head down, I stepped in, thinking this is more than I can bear.
When I raised my head, there sat a man with no legs, smiling at me from a wheelchair.

How ya doing, he said with a smile? Man, it's a beautiful day!!
Startled, I mumbled something like fine; I guess I'm ok.

We reached the ground floor, and I held the elevator door as his wife pushed him into the hall.
He grinned, said thanks a lot, be careful, and God bless you, my friend, as I recall.

Suddenly I stood up a little straighter, had less pain, gone were the woe is me thoughts I was having before.
I walked to the car, silently thanking God, and though I will probably fail, try not to feel sorry for myself anymore.

Crutches, Walkers, and Handrails

In my youth, lots of things occupied my mind as I traveled life's highways, roads, and trails.
However, I can truthfully say that I gave little, if any, thought to crutches, walkers, or handrails.

As I age and go through operations, my steps tend to become unsteady and slow.
And in the past ten years these items, have, at times, come to my aid wherever I would go.

Knee replacements brought out the walker, and in a crowd, it gave me the protection of bars.
In the mall, people gave me a wide berth, and outside folks saw me better and slowed down in their cars.

Crutches were a different story. People seemed annoyed like I was always in their way.
It's hard to dodge little kids, and I even had a woman knock one of them down in Sam's Club one day.

She didn't say I'm sorry, are you all right, offer to pick up the crutch, or anything at all.
She just looked like I should not be in her way, no concern that she almost made me fall.

Ahh, handrails, thank God for them! They have saved me time after time.
Just not enough of them in places I go these days, where I have to climb.

Aside from the handrails nowadays, I don't need the other two.
But we all need to be courteous and watch out for those that do.

Breakdown Blues

Now you and I know that autos, appliances, and such do just what they are programmed to do.
They are inanimate objects, no heart, no soul, no ability to think things through.

Yet someway, somehow over the years, and how they discern this I do not know,
The car breaks down, the refrigerator goes out, just when you think you've got a little extra dough.

You get a bonus check from work, or the income tax refund finally comes in.
Before you can tell your wife, she calls and says the water heater is leaking again.

Now to revisit what I was saying before, and even though it may sound funny,
Those things we have that make our lives comfortable, somehow know to break when you have extra money.

A check is coming from Washington, I am told. Virus money they call it, but I haven't got mine yet.
Twelve hundred dollars will soon be in my account. Seems no one worries anymore about the national debt.

But you know how much I'm going to clear? Thirty dollars. Not enough for a good dinner downtown.
Why you ask, I'll tell you why. Because one of our two air conditioning units went down.

Now our good friend Travis fixed the darn thing, did an excellent job, and cut us a break.
But it goes to show you what I've said before; repairs will take any extra you make.

My wife, always the practical one, says, be thankful we didn't have to get into the savings account.
I am, but I wish just one time, I could get me a bonus without car trouble or an appliance going out.

Diane and Teresa

Divorce. The word just seems to tear at one's heart.
Those once joined together as man and wife, now torn apart.

It's happened in our close-knit family to Tommy and Bobby, our sons.
Both almost reached the twenty-year mark before their marriages became undone.

So, while Margaret and I never had girls of our own,
We welcomed Diane and Teresa, just like daughters, into our home.

Tommy was married to Teresa; Bobby was married to Diane.
We were very saddened when both marriages came to an end.

However, God always knows what's best, and I'm happy to say,
All parted on good terms, no animosity, and are good friends to this day.

Diane is in nursing, loves the Nashville Predators, and spending time with family and friends.
Teresa, the mother of our Grandson Aaron, is in banking, estate planning, and has married again.

When divorce happens, like these situations prove, it's not always an unhappy thing.
Sometimes problems arise, and parting ways can make life right again.

While we welcome the two new loves that our sons have found,
We do miss the many times that Diane and Teresa came around.

Over the years, they became like the daughters we never had.
But we thank God that so much good came from what could have been so bad.

And I believe both of our ex daughters-in-law since their divorces have known,
That we love them, miss them, and they are always welcome in our home.

Our Class

How does one thank God enough for those they have known for seventy years?
Classmates, friends, husbands, wives, and others they hold dear?

It's an impossible task, but the Harris High Class of 1961 certainly try.
We gather each September in Spruce Pine, NC, as another year goes by.

We just met last Saturday again, and many classmates said this Reunion was one of our best.
I agree, but somehow, this time seemed different from all the rest.

Maybe it's because I'm getting old, hard to get around, facing my mortality.
But as I looked around the room, I realized just how dear these classmates are to me.

I thought of how 109 of us started so young and strong in 1949,
How the world had changed and the things we had seen happen in our time!

I paused by the pictures of the deceased classmates displayed for us to see.
Placed my hands on some of them and wondered, why not me?

Of the 109 that started with us in the first grade, forty have passed away.
I don't know how God works things out, but somehow, I felt their presence there that day.

We had lost two since we held our last Reunion one year ago.
The last one having passed away just in the prior week or so.

Oh, don't get me wrong. A great time was had all around.
Laughing, talking, not a sad face to be found.

It's a fantastic thing that happens, and each year I see it occur.
The older we get and the more we tell it, in our mind, the better we were.

I am so glad our Class has held together, that everyone feels they are an important part.
And they are. To me, each one is special, like family, very close to my heart.

Well, time (as our age shows) moves on, and we have to say goodbye to classmates we hold so dear.
May God in His mercy grant us all health and safety until we return next year.

The Committee

In this somber year of the dreaded Coronavirus and the risks for folks in their seventies, fun, by necessity, must wait.
Although it's April and the Harris High Class of 1961 Reunion is not until the last of September, The Committee wonders if we should cancel or set a later date.

It's a dilemma for those of us on The Committee for more reasons than one.
We had rather not cancel because missing a year, at our age, means more Class members may be gone.

On the other hand, holding it this year in marginal conditions, and folks get sick, or something goes wrong,
Then we've defeated the purpose we were striving for, and still have some of us move on.

So, The Committee met by electronic means, each one having their input, impartial, and fair.
The consensus was to wait until mid-July, check things out, and decide how to proceed from there.

This decision got me thinking about how I had taken The Committee for granted over the years.
The hard work, time, effort, phone calls, and yes, some out of pocket cash if a shortage appeared.

I know I speak for The Committee when I say each Class Member is important no matter the name.
But I think when our Class History is written, not to name and thank The Committee would be a shame.

The chairperson is Doris, with Elaine as her steady right hand. Tommy and Eddie Jo made most of the calls.
Danny, Troy, and Roy, our treasurer's, are always available for whatever needs doing. David is our historian, and Doug keeps us legal and all.

I serve on The Committee even though I live 300 miles away and can't personally meet.
We communicate by email and text, and at the Reunions occasionally, I will speak.

So, there you have it, Class, the hard-working folks that make everything fall in place, the ones that deserve our thanks.
Because believe me, fellow classmates, things don't just happen, and that you can take to the bank.

What Do You Do??

I received the worst possible news in a text the other day,
From my best friend of fifty years, that now lives several states away.

We worked together, fished together, and he is closer than a brother can be.
Cancer, he said, only months to live, he said, this was the sad news he sent to me.

What does one do? What can I do? My best friend lies in Texas, dying.
Every time I think of him and pray for him, I can hardly stop crying.

I'm no stranger to death; at my age, it's all around me.
And as a wise man once said, "Death runs in my family."

So, I'll pray for him, ask others to, and try to help though far away.
I'll call him, we will talk about the old days, but I just can't do it today.

What can I do, I keep asking myself, I always knew this day would come,
To one of us because we are both seventy years old and then some.

It's the circle of life. We live, we love, raise our families, laugh, and cry.
Love our neighbors, care for each other, serve God, then we die.

Still, as I write this about my friend, I wish there were something I could do,
To change the situation, or make him feel better with a comforting word or two.

But about all I can do is lift him up to our Savior and comfort him until the end.
And rest in the assurance of knowing that one day soon, I will join my friend.

Why Not Me?

The circle of life. The wheel spins. Life goes on. What's new is old, what's old is new in our journey.
Clichés' abound as life winds down, and one contemplates what's ahead for you and me.

Growing up, it was the old folks dying, and it seemed I was dragged to a funeral every week or two.
Now that I'm in the old folk's category about every few weeks, guess what, it's déjà vu.

Last year we counted over forty people we knew that passed away.
We didn't go to all the funerals, of course, but we averaged about two every twenty-eight days.

I heard a minister once say that death runs in the family, and this we know is a guarantee.
It's an unwelcome visitor in all families, and one day will knock on the door for you and me.

And I began thinking when a dear, dear friend answered that knock and left us last June.
What about you (me), big boy? Will that unwelcome visitor be at your door soon?

Like the old folks of my youth, I now stand at the graveside of many friends that from this life are now set free.
And looking back at my misspent youth, my failures and sins, I have to wonder, why not me?

Why am I still here I ponder as I watch good friends, good people as they are laid to rest?
Many are classmates, coworkers, neighbors, and family members that always rose to the test.

And here I am already missing them, mourning their passing, and trying to figure things out.
We start the process of dying the day we are born, so why are we so surprised when this day comes about?

Then, inevitably that little voice inside, you know, that persistent convicting voice we sometimes ignore,
Saying it's not My time for you yet. I've got things for you to do. I will call you on My timetable, not one minute before.

I know, at 77 years of age, my time will come to answer deaths knock at the door.
I am ready to go; and I have no real fear. Still, I'm glad that the hour, time, and place I don't know.

One thing is for sure as I stroll down the path of what's left of my earthly time.
I've traveled a pleasant road, and it's a safe bet I have fewer sunsets ahead than I do behind.

We must soldier on, trust in God, help our struggling fellowman by doing our best to end poverty.
Keeping in mind that the only Jesus some people will ever see. . .they see in you and me.

Hope to meet you on the other side.

See You Soon

We started school together. I remember I sat beside you in either the third or fourth grade.
We played on the playground together, rode the school bus, enjoyed being young and unafraid.

In the middle school years, we began to stretch our wings, broaden our horizons, so to speak.
Still, we were friends, studying, looking forward, with hormones about to peak.

Then came the high school years, some of the best years of our lives, up until then.
Sports and activities, teachers that prepared us for adulthood, that was soon to begin.

Memories are plentiful, of dates, football games, and just hanging out.
Trips, parties, a little mischief here and there that we won't talk about.

We had the world by the tail, thinking the ride would never end.
And even after graduation, we kept in touch and were friends.

Now, I stand here beside your grave, crying, trying to understand, and asking why,
Knowing that from the moment of our first breath, it's then that we begin to die.

That doesn't make it any easier, though, my dear classmate and friend, now that your days on earth are through.
However, as the circle of life comes around, and it always does, soon, I will be joining you.

What's the Purpose of It All?

An old man sat in the park, not very far from his home.
Lost in memories and thoughts, he sat all alone.

Not far away, children were playing, running to, and fro.
A tear ran down the man's face as he wondered, "where did the time go?"

A mother called to her child, "be careful, don't fall,"
The old man thought, what's the purpose of it all?

He had worked all his life, done the best that he could,
Two sons that were grown, they had both turned out good.

He had played by the rules, been honest, always worked,
Loved God, family, country, always went to church.

But now, as he sat there, he had never felt so old.
Age, occupation, operations, and arthritis had taken their toll.

As he watched the children play, he tried to recall,
When he felt that good, but he couldn't at all.

Suddenly a chic elderly lady and a toddler drew near.
It was his grandson and his wife of these many, many years.

The old man's demeanor suddenly changed, he had a big smile,
He felt a lot better, stood up straighter than he had in a while.

The three of them walked away together, hand in hand in hand,
Laughing, talking, life now was so grand.

The old man feeling, a touch of shame for his thoughts,
Silently began to thank God for all of life's blessings He had brought.

I know this really happened you see,
Because the old man in this story is none other than me.

The Wisdom of the Cherokee

(Several people claim this story, so the idea is not mine,

only as it is written in poetry.)

A young Cherokee boy of about twelve was sitting at his Grandfather's knee one day.
He asked his Grandfather about life and how a man got to be that way.

The old warrior smiled and said, you have to control the wolves, my son.
Puzzled, the young brave said, but Grandfather, that cannot be done.

His Grandfather said I do not mean the wolves that run wild,
I mean, the wolves that have been in you since you were a child.

Sadly, the young man thought some evil spirit is in my Grandfather's head.
Sensing his grandson's confusion, the Grandfather quietly said,

You see, my young brave when you are born two wolves also move in.
One is good. The other is evil, and they inhabit your body until the end.

No matter where you are, the battle can continue in many ways.
These wolves often rob you of sleep and alter what you do each day.

Grandfather the young man said, which one of these wolves wins in this fight you say our bodies host??
The wise Grandfather smiled and took his grandson's hand in his and said: My son, the one fed the most.

Contemplation

I find that in the fast-paced world we live in today,
It's getting harder and harder to get away.

Oh, I don't mean to take a vacation or go on a long trip.
Or go to some faraway island on an airplane or a ship.

No, what I'm talking about is more complicated than an island to find.
It's a quiet place you can go for an hour or two and free up your mind.

Often amid the noise of the city with sirens, traffic, and ringing of phones,
I feel the need, if only for an hour, to be somewhere quiet and alone.

From my home in Murfreesboro, fortunately, it is not very far,
To Stones River Battlefield, where a battle was fought in the Civil War.

It covers several hundred acres of trails, roads, cedar trees, and streams.
And most of the time, one can find a spot peaceful and serene.

I've parked looking out over meadows where soldiers from both North and South fought and bled.
And sat on the hillside where the good people of Murfreesboro buried hundreds of the dead.

I've thought of how in the books on the Battle it had been said,
That the fighting was so brutal, the Stones River ran red.

Soon, before I know it, hours have gone by, and more often than not, I begin to pray.
It's hard to explain, but the problems that had troubled and brought me there, start to slip away.

Somehow, I am changed when I spend some quiet time on that sacred sod.
I come away with new hope, a different outlook, and feeling a lot closer to God.

No Tears

I sit by the window in my living room, watching the leaves of October fall on the grass.
In silence, I wonder after seventy-six years if this change of season will be my last.

Oh, I'm feeling ok, I can walk, talk, do some physical work, although sometimes with a bit of pain.
My brain still works, I'm blessed in many ways, and I try my best not to complain.

But like the seasons' change and winter follows fall at this time every year,
I can feel my life changing, steps getting slower, my winter is drawing near.

I used to worry about my departure, think about it, try to put it out of my mind.
I don't worry anymore; live each day to its fullest; try to make good use of my time.

You see, I made my peace with my Savior as a boy, and He has been with me all these years.
So as my departure draws near, I would ask one favor of those who love me:
Shed no tears.

I've had a great life from beginning to end, been blessed by God above,
Known pleasure and pain, sunshine and rain, and love, love, love.

My wife and family have been the very best any man could ever imagine or dreamed.
Friends, mentors, and so many others crossed my path at just the right time it always seemed.

I never thought I would live this long, figuring around forty I would meet my fate.
Just goes to show you Who is in charge, and He alone determines that date.

You know that when I'm in Heaven with Jesus, there are many old friends I'll see.
Celebrate my departure with laughter and singing, but shed no tears for me.

I hope everyone makes their plans to come to my new Home because that is where I will be.
On earth, have a ball, love, and care for each other. And think of, but please don't shed any tears for me.

Acknowledgements

To Margaret, my wife, who encouraged me, and gave me ideas for the cover. Thank you for your support along the way. Tommy and Bobby, our sons, and Grandson Aaron, who helped decide book themes while sitting around the supper table during our weekly Monday gatherings. Also, thank you for tirelessly listening to my poems and providing your opinions. Thanks to Bob for the work on the early manuscript.

Tommy and Faye Biddix, my parents, who helped form who I am. Helen and Burl Willis, my in-laws, who treated me as their son and welcomed me into their family. I was blessed to grow up in the beautiful Blue Ridge Mountains of Western North Carolina during the time I did.

Johnny Simmons, my first cousin, shared many adventures with me. You are like a brother.

WD and Jackie Thomason, longtime friends, who I could always count on for prayer and an uplifting word. My lifetime friend, Larry Boyd, with whom so many memories are shared. My friend, coworker, and fishing partner, DP (Dave) Davis, who tragically passed away in 2019.

Harris High Class of 1961 classmates, you are the best! Together we began our journey in the first grade, continuing until graduation. Our subsequent class reunions have kept us close at heart.

Lastly, words cannot express enough thanks to my cousin, Rosalie Lowery-Abell, who gave so much of her time to this effort. Without her tireless work in editing, encouragement, gentle criticism, and suggestions, this book would have never been possible.

To all who spoke a kind word, many I have written about, friends, classmates, coworkers, and those I met along the way, I thank you.

God bless you all!

Author Bio

ET Biddix has the ability to involve the reader in every phase of his life as if they were walking with him. His life story is written in verse in Looking Beyond the Rearview Mirror. He describes his early life in the Blue Ridge Mountains, through the ups and downs of the school years, marriage, family, work years, and into retirement. Along the way, you meet famous people (Ali, Marty Robbins, and others) and his many friends.

ET is brutally honest, yet able to laugh at himself, and provide some common-sense advice for us today. You learn of his faith, struggles, and triumphs, all with a unique blend of fact and humor.

While Looking Beyond the Rearview Mirror is one person's story, a thread of nostalgia, life lessons, and hope for tomorrow that is common to us all is present. So, settle back, take a look back at the past, live for today, and look to the future!

Contact: etbiddix@aol.com

My dad, Tommy Biddix, Standing Right

Grandparents, John and Lula Lowery

Tommy Biddix – 1943

Parents, Tommy and Faye Lowery Biddix

Dad and Me
(He called me Skip)

The House Where I Was Raised

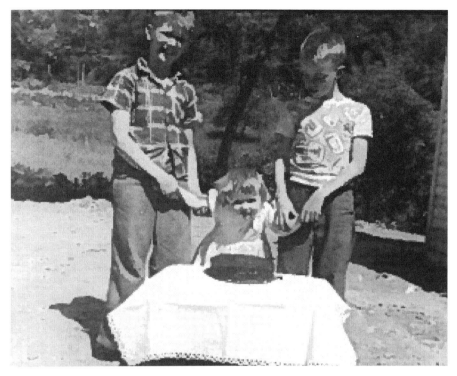

Me, My Sister Polly, and First Cousin John Simmons

Edwin Tommy Biddix - 1961

Margaret Alice Willis - 1961

Football 1960

Larry Boyd – Football 1960

Larry Boyd – Lifetime Friend

DP (Dave) Davis and Wife Jan
(Friend and Fishing Partner for 40 Years, Now Deceased)

WD Thomason
Friend of 48 Years

Aaron Morgan Biddix (Grandson)
Baseball 2007

Aaron Today

E.T. Biddix – Present Day

Margaret Biddix – Present Day

Left to Right: Bobby, Tommy, Aaron, Margaret, Ed

The Ladies – Erica, Margaret, Liene

*Ed and Margaret
Christmas Eve, 2019*

Made in the USA
Columbia, SC
17 September 2020